The Accessible Music Classroom for All

The Accessible Music Classroom for All

by
Brian J. Wagner-Yeung

Foreword by
Elise S. Sobol

ROWMAN & LITTLEFIELD
Lanham • Boulder • New York • London
Published in cooperation with the National Association for Music Education.

Rowman & Littlefield
Bloomsbury Publishing Inc, 1385 Broadway, New York, NY 10018, USA
Bloomsbury Publishing Plc, 50 Bedford Square, London, WC1B 3DP, UK
Bloomsbury Publishing Ireland, 29 Earlsfort Terrace, Dublin 2, D02 AY28, Ireland
www.rowman.com

Copyright © 2025 by The Rowman & Littlefield Publishing Group, Inc.

All rights reserved. No part of this publication may be: i) reproduced or transmitted in any form, electronic or mechanical, including photocopying, recording or by means of any information storage or retrieval system without prior permission in writing from the publishers; or ii) used or reproduced in any way for the training, development or operation of artificial intelligence (AI) technologies, including generative AI technologies. The rights holders expressly reserve this publication from the text and data mining exception as per Article 4(3) of the Digital Single Market Directive (EU) 2019/790.

British Library Cataloguing in Publication Information Available

Library of Congress Cataloging-in-Publication Data

Names: Wagner-Yeung, Brian J., 1983- author. | Sobol, Elise S., writer of foreword.
Title: The accessible music classroom for all / by Brian J. Wagner-Yeung; foreword by Elise S. Sobol.
Description: Lanham : Rowman & Littlefield Publishers, 2025. |
 Includes bibliographical references and index.
Summary: "This book provides teachers with the tools to give every student the appropriate support needed in music classrooms, especially in diverse settings, by presenting evidence-based strategies and examples of accessible music-making in action. While the book focuses on students with disabilities, readers will find that the strategies can benefit all"—Provided by publisher.
Identifiers: LCCN 2024052608 (print) | LCCN 2024052609 (ebook) |
 ISBN 9798881807092 (cloth) | ISBN 9798881807108 (paperback) |
 ISBN 9798881807115 (ebook)
Subjects: LCSH: Children with disabilities—Education. | Music—Instruction and study. | Inclusive education.
Classification: LCC MT17 .W25 2025 (print) | LCC MT17 (ebook) |
 DDC 371.9/04487—dc23/eng/20241106
LC record available at https://lccn.loc.gov/2024052608
LC ebook record available at https://lccn.loc.gov/2024052609

For product safety related questions contact productsafety@bloomsbury.com.

∞™ The paper used in this publication meets the minimum requirements of American National Standard for Information Sciences—Permanence of Paper for Printed Library Materials, ANSI/NISO Z39.48-1992.

Contents

Acknowledgments		vii
Foreword		xi
Preface		xv
1	Access for ALL?	1
2	Who Is ALL?	11
3	Who Shapes the Strength-Based Environment?	29
4	What Are the Basic Ideas?	45
5	How Do We Make Accessible Music for ALL?	61
6	How Do We Enhance Lifelong Learning in the Process for ALL?	87
7	How Do We Create an Accessible, Strength-Based, Structured, and Predictable Learning Environment?	117
8	Why?	143
Appendix A: Sample Lesson Activities		151
Appendix B: Suggested Resources		161
Index		165
About the Author		171

Acknowledgments

When I announced I wanted to start this project, I casually recall mentioning it to Dr. Elise Sobol somewhere between Rochester and Syracuse on the New York Thruway, driving back from the 2023 NAfME Eastern Division Conference. By the end of the conversation, she had convinced me I was ready to do this. With Elise's blessing and guidance, I am happy that this day has arrived.

On that account, I would first like to recognize and thank Dr. Elise Sobol. I first met Elise at the 2012 NYSSMA® Winter Conference when she was in the role of Music for Special Learners Chair for NYSSMA®. I randomly approached her in the conference hall lobby to introduce myself and mention that I had learned much throughout the sessions she presided over. By the end of the conversation, she had inspired me to submit a session proposal for the following year. I heeded her advice with a colleague, Gina Costanza, and we presented our first session, *Inclusive Music Teaching: Exceeding the Standards,* at the following conference. Throughout the process, Elise provided endless support and was our guiding star. She took the time to meet in person with us multiple times in Queens to help us (even at a Starbucks). Fast-forward through the years, and nothing has changed in Elise's approach. She has supported every decision in my career, and I could not be more grateful for having her as a friend and a mentor. She sees the best in everyone and helps them find a pathway to achieve their dreams. I hope this work helps support the remarkable legacy she continues to build and share, bettering the lives of everyone she meets.

Thank you to the team at NYSSMA®. I am thankful for the opportunities to collaborate with the different committees and the support from our fabulous leadership as I am finishing up my fourth year as Neurodiversity and Accessibility Chair. I am also thankful for having the opportunity to impact positive change across New York. Thank you to (listed alphabetically) Shelly Bauer, Adele Bovard, Dr. David Brown, Michael Brownell, Edmund Chiarello, Russ Faunce, Thomas Gellert, Marc Green, Dr. Keith Koster, Terry Nigrelli, Kathy Perconti, Daryle Redmond, Michael Robertson, Michael Salzman, Maria Schwab, and George Smith.

Thank you to Riki Braunstein and Marianne Gythfeldt for bringing me on as faculty at CUNY Brooklyn College. You have put your faith in me to help shape the next generation of music teachers, and I am eternally grateful for the opportunity. A special recognition goes out to all the undergrad and grad students I have taught over the last several years. You are part of our music education family now.

Thank you to the leaders in our field of music education. Some have personally taught me, some I have had the luxury to watch at conferences, and others I have absorbed your resources to help better myself. You inspire me to be my best, and I am so grateful for your extraordinary contributions to our field. Thank you to (listed alphabetically) Dr. Mary Adamek, Dr. Cindy Bell, Dr. Cara Bernard, Dr. Rhoda Bernard, Dr. Alice-Ann Darrow, Dr. Susan Davis, Dr. Rachel Grimsby, Dr. Alice Hammel, Dr. Ryan Hourigan, Dr. Judith Jellison, Dr. Kim McCord, Dr. Constance McKoy, and Dr. Janice Smith.

Thank you to the fabulous music educators I have met over the years. Your work has inspired me in so many ways. Some of you helped support my transition from the start of my career into leadership, and others I have watched shape new ways that will help change our field for the better. Thank you to (listed alphabetically) Maureen Butler, Christopher Cavarretta, Gina Costanza, Krysta Mirsik DePuy, Dr. Angela Guerriero, Elizabeth Guglielmo, Dr. Christopher Hanson, Jessica Kimple, Jennifer Schecter-Lonborg, Marie Malara, Amanda McFee, Cody Messersmith, Barbara Murray, Barbara Novick, Patti Peltz, Katherine Stock, Peter Tinaglia, and Michelle Turner. A special acknowledgment to all the New York City Public Schools arts educators and leaders I have met over the years.

Acknowledgments

Thank you to the fabulous music educators who inspired my love for music, and my pathway for education in my childhood. Special recognition to Linda Shubert, Laura Knudsen, Maria Wingert, John Myszka, Erika Felker, and Ingrid DeMilo.

Thank you to the organizations and non-profits I have collaborated with over the years. A special shoutout to the Office of Accessibility and VSA at The Kennedy Center, the Council for Exceptional Children Division of Visual and Performing Arts Education (DARTS), Just Say Hi! through the Cerebral Palsy Foundation (CPF), and Music ConstructED.

Thank you to the DREAM TEAM arts department that highlights what solid teamwork represents—Melissa Carlin and Diane McCarthy. We went from just *figuring it out as we go along* to *rocking it*. I could not have done it without you. Thank you to Alexandra Ponzetto and Jaclyn Santana for being my official first-draft readers, giving continuous support, and reminding me that what we are doing matters. Thank you to my administration at P370K and Brooklyn School of Inquiry, and special recognition goes out to all the students I have taught over the years. This is for you.

Thank you to the folks at NAfME and Rowman & Littlefield, who helped support this dream. Thank you to Amy Bradley, Catherina Hurlburt, Michael Tan, Hollis Peterson, and Taylor Breeding.

And finally, a special thank-you to my family. To my wonderful husband David, my mom, and my extended family in Hawaii and Vancouver. You have supported me throughout the years as I try to make a mark in this world. I could not be more grateful.

Foreword

Whether teacher, professor, or mentor, one of the greatest joys of our profession is seeing one's protégé evolve to become an influential change maker in the field. And so it is with Brian Wagner-Yeung.

Twelve years ago, Brian introduced himself to me at the New York State School Music Association (NYSSMA®) Winter Conference in Rochester, New York, after attending the Music for Special Learners sessions that I chaired. Expanding my outreach as a resource to music teachers across the state was always of paramount importance to me. It was my pleasure to meet and subsequently offer guidance and support to Brian Wagner-Yeung in his career path. Throughout the years of our collaborations, it was with great delight that I saw his career take hold, build, and impact others.

I always kept in the back of my mind the need for someone who could continue the service work at the state level that I started more than thirty years ago while a public-school music teacher at the Nassau BOCES Department of Special Education. Such great progress had been made not only stateside, but nationally, too. For example, to make a connection to *The Accessible Music Classroom for All*, I would like to share that in the 2012 National Association for Music Education (NAfME) Music in Our Schools Month broadcast, a video clip of my Rosemary Kennedy High School choir students was selected to sing the "The Star-Spangled Banner." Viewers across the nation saw for the *first* time students with intellectual and developmental disabilities including autism spectrum disorders singing our national anthem's closing words, "the land of the free, and home of the brave." This milestone broadcast across America showcased that ALL our students, including students with intellectual and developmental disabilities, were a part of our "land of the free, and home of the brave." Bravo to the National Association for Music Education!

Needless to say, as I was approaching retirement from teaching at Nassau BOCES, recommending the right successor to serve as state chair was key to continuing the advocacy for music inclusion for our students with disabilities. Fast-forward, with passion and drive, now as the New York State School Music Association state chair for neurodiversity and accessibility, Brian has taken up the mantle. He is an emerging visionary leader, an active international clinician, a dedicated music teacher to hundreds of students who through the years needed varying levels of support for their school success, and a passionate collegiate instructor earnest in his desire to help preservice music teachers prepare ALL their future students to have a sense of welcome, belonging, and access to a high-quality music education.

For those who cannot personally visit Brian Wagner-Yeung's music classroom, college classes, or conference sessions, *The Accessible Music Classroom for All* effectively and most vividly encapsulates his principles and process. The book is beautifully written and organized. He talks to the reader as if he were conversing face-to-face. Designed as a teacher's practical guide to music learning, we as readers are prompted, through his naturally dynamic and welcoming style, to engage in self-reflection, ensuring that our work is centered on the needs of ALL the students we teach.

Many qualities of the book make *The Accessible Music Classroom for All* so user-friendly. The eight chapters in the volume can each stand alone, yet they flow one to the other with the joy of learning together. Each chapter is framed by an essential question section, followed by core vocabulary specific to the chapter, then the new content, and a summary with closing comments. Every chapter is written through the teaching approach of universal design for learning (UDL), demonstrated through the wide variety of learning styles of the featured students.

Each chapter offers a wealth of insights that readers can implement promptly in their music program or adapt to their individual teaching setting. I favor chapter 5: "How Do We Make Music Accessible for All?" The music content teacher will find the examples for differentiating instruction incredibly helpful. At the end of the book are resources to guide readers for further study. The index helps with cross referencing.

Whether teaching in a general education class or designated special education class, every teaching strategy the author suggests can be generalized across contexts in inclusive settings for studio teaching, classroom, instrumental or vocal performance programs. Key ideas that flow throughout the book also cover current educational issues. Brian discusses access, belonging, bias-free practices, neurodiversity, equity, inclusion, and social justice while showcasing standards-based lessons where his students engage in the artistic processes of creating, performing, presenting, producing; responding, and connecting through culturally relevant repertoire.

Brian has written this very personal yet very practical book for ALL of US at whatever stage we are in our careers. His breadth of text is concise yet comprehensive. As he has written in his opening self-reflection, he hopes that the text will be "insightful, resourceful, practical, inspirational, and valuable." I can honestly say that the book is all those descriptors and more. It is time to celebrate!

The Accessible Music Classroom for All is a wonderful addition to our field. Informative and written from the heart with invaluable experiences shared, *The Accessible Music Classroom for All* will make a difference to music teachers everywhere.

Elise S. Sobol, EdD
Faculty, NYU Steinhardt, Department of Music and Performing Arts Professions
Faculty, LIU Post College of Education, Department of Educational Leadership
Rowman & Littlefield author

Preface

I can remember my first year of teaching as if it were yesterday. During the first week, I vividly recall teaching only kindergarten and first-grade students in an oversized room with high-school furniture; teaching a kindergarten class of students who only spoke Mandarin with no adult assistance; teaching many self-contained classes of nonspeaking students, and having no idea what to do; ALL while settling into a new career and building my own program from nothing with barely any materials. Several weeks later, feeling defeated, I considered whether I wanted to be a teacher. I had gone through a fantastic teacher preparation program, but how was I not prepared to teach such a range of learners? How was there no time in our coursework to prepare these needed tools? Does this sound like you?

Fast-forward sixteen years, and here I am writing this book. Nevertheless, it was a journey to get here. It started through attending many professional developments over the years, exposing me to teaching strategies for students with disabilities; reading much of the existing literature to gain knowledge and strategies to apply in my classroom; collaborating with other teachers to share ideas; and pursuing an advanced certificate degree to gain a more in-depth understanding. But then it eventually transitioned to presenting my own workshops at conferences and publishing articles; teaching preservice educators in a collegiate setting; taking on leadership roles within the New York State School Music Association (NYSSMA®) and elsewhere; and, most importantly, watching my students become independent and empowered citizens through music. I slowly realized that what I was doing was working, and now it was my turn to share how.

And this brings us to *The Accessible Music Classroom for All*. One of the main areas of feedback I hear when I give a presentation is that how I showcase my ideas is *practical*. This is the exact goal I want this book to achieve. Over the years, I have been exposed to exceptional leaders in accessible music education and have incorporated their ideas into my teaching practice. My goal with this text is to combine ALL those ideas, put them into a practical lens, and show you what it looks like. Then, you can take it away and incorporate it into your setting.

I acknowledge that I know you will ALL come from different perspectives. Some of you will be preservice educators, taking coursework on the pathway to your teaching certification. Some will already be in the field looking for resources, ideas, strategies, affirmation, or help. Some may be in additional roles, such as administrators, collegiate faculty, teaching artists, music therapists, teaching privately or in studios, nonprofit or arts education organizations, or elsewhere. No matter what your role is, this book is for you. I am writing from the viewpoint that the audience is a wide range of learners, and you will come to this with various levels of training, knowledge, and preparation.

When considering the key ideas, I wanted to focus on evidence-based strategies with research behind them for support. In my travels, I often hear teachers needing guidance when teaching a diverse range of learners simultaneously. Therefore, that is the angle from which this text is coming. Although we will focus mainly on students with disabilities or students with the most needs, we will explore how these strategies benefit ALL students. This is why the most critical word in this text is *ALL*. There is a reason you will see this word capitalized throughout the entire book. That is because these strategies work for ALL. We will focus on universal design for learning (UDL), multisensory learning, assistive technology, task analysis, and conceptual learning—while approaching everything from a strength-based model for ALL.

This text will be organized by answering the following basic Wh-questions: *who, what, where, why,* and *how*. We start by focusing on ourselves and self-reflecting on where the current trends in music education and our field stand. We then focus on *who* the students are in our classrooms and using up-to-date language and terminology to describe them. Next, we focus on the adults *who* engage with our students. In addition, we also focus on the biases we have and how they impact our classrooms. Then, we move on to *what* the evidence-based strategies are and go into detail about what they mean.

Moving forward, we use an entire chapter to focus on *how* this looks in the music classroom (e.g., music literacy, singing, listening, composition, playing instruments, and musical theater/ensembles). Then, we move on to *how* music impacts lifelong learning for ALL, mainly focusing on language and communication, social skills, self-esteem, social emotional learning, emotional regulation, and developing independence. We next move to a chapter focused on the classroom environment, *where* we specifically include students with sensory, medical, and physical needs. We also focus a chunk of time on the function of behavior and developing strategies to replace targeted behaviors. We close by self-reflecting again, asking ourselves *why* this is important, and discussing the following steps to move ourselves forward.

One unique aspect of this text is that I provide numerous examples of what this ALL looks like. Too often, we do not get to connect as educators and see high-quality, standards-based examples of making music in action for a diverse range of learners. Moreover, many may need help applying this new information in their classrooms. In this text, I provide concrete examples coming from my own classroom. In addition to the examples throughout the text, one appendix specifically focuses on sample lesson ideas and a second provides a list of resources for you.

I hope you find this text practical, engaging, supportive, beneficial, and accessible. My goal is to help fill in the gaps in our field and training and to help you become more confident in creating accessible classrooms for ALL. I also hope this text will help pave the way for a future generation of accessible music education leaders to expand our field further.

Together, let us break down barriers and make the world a welcome place for ALL.

Chapter 1

Access for ALL?

ESSENTIAL QUESTIONS

1. What are the overarching ideas of an accessible music classroom for ALL?
2. How can music educators recognize potential barriers in the learning environment, teacher delivery, or academic content?

CORE VOCABULARY

Shaping, access, inclusion, barriers, exclusion, belonging, welcome, ALL

OPENING THOUGHTS: SELF-REFLECTION

Welcome to *The Accessible Music Classroom for ALL*. I hope you find this text insightful, resourceful, practical, inspirational, and valuable. This book will be a journey that covers many topics, strategies, and ideas that may be familiar or new. My goal in writing this text is to break down some existing obstacles in our field of music education and help make it more accessible and inclusive for ALL. Although this text will mainly focus on strategies for the students we teach, part of it also has to do with us—the adults.

Before we embark on our journey, I invite you to engage in a self-reflection activity. This is an assignment I do with my college students at the start of every semester. The purpose of this activity is to encourage you to reflect on your own personal and professional journey and to assess your current stance on various aspects of education. There are no right or wrong answers here. We are ALL unique individuals at different stages of our careers, so please do not feel pressured. Just take a moment to reflect and imagine how you would respond to these questions in a face-to-face conversation.

Think about the following:

1. Who are you personally and musically? How would you describe your background, identity, interests, upbringing, and strengths? Do these impact you as a teacher?
2. How do you learn something best? In what ways do you acquire a new skill? Do you think the way you learn is like how others learn? How so?
3. Do ALL students have the same opportunities? How so? What impacts your answer to this?
4. How do you feel about teaching a wide range of learners? What do you think about teaching and engaging students who have disabilities? What is your approach to teaching students who may learn differently? What challenges arise in teaching an array of learners?

As mentioned, there are no correct answers to these questions. At the end of this text, you will do a similar activity where you will reflect on your growth. These questions may sound simple, but they are essential to consider. These four questions are interconnected and directly impact our teaching and, therefore, student success. Who we are as teachers and our pathways to this moment directly affect how we teach and view our students.

A significant part of this book will involve dismantling our current approaches and forging new pathways in teaching and connecting with our students. I understand that this journey may sometimes be uncomfortable or lead to disagreements. That is perfectly normal. As I will reiterate throughout this book, we are ALL human beings, part of the same genus and species. However, to evolve, we must be willing to reevaluate what we believe and how we teach.

MY STORY

To be fair, I should probably do the same activity and share with you. I am a white, cisgender male, in my early forties, part of the LGBTQIA2S+ community, also with a non-apparent disability. I grew up in a single-parent household in Long Island, New York—and now reside in Queens, New York City, with my husband. I am a classically trained cellist and have performed in multiple ensembles in the New York City region. I have taught music in a center-based special education public-school program in New York City for the past fifteen years. I received my music education training at CUNY Queens College.

When I learn something new, I am a visual and kinesthetic learner. I learn best by watching or practicing something (e.g., watching a YouTube video, reading about it, or watching someone else model it). When someone explains directions to me verbally, I tend to zone out. Imagine what that was like growing up as a student in public schools, where the teaching practice was mainly dictating notes for us to copy.

When I consider teaching a wide range of learners, because I have mainly taught in a special education setting most of my career, I feel passionate about it. However, it took me many years to get where I am now. I can admit now that at first I had many biases about my students and their capabilities. It took years for me to break these down and see my students as the wonderful, capable human beings I see today.

How I feel about teaching children with disabilities directly connects to the previous paragraph. Unfortunately, my teacher training program did not fully prepare me to teach a wide range of learners. I had excellent professors who prepared me for many other aspects of music education. However, the program did not allow time or coursework to thoroughly discuss students who learn and experience the world differently—more on this to come.

In the college class that I teach currently, I call this assignment an opening statement. As mentioned, the focus is self-reflection on where we currently stand. I wish I could go back fifteen years, do the same assignment, and see what I would have answered then. I can only guess what my feelings were and recall memories and teaching situations where I felt a lack of preparation.

As human beings who enter the teaching force, we are ALL shaped by how and where we were raised and trained to be educators. I like to use the word **shaping** because in my mind, I imagine us like clay pottery. Different hands mold us at various times in our creation, which impacts the overall shape that we eventually become. It is similar to the way we become teachers and grow as human beings. Our students ALL go through the same process.

Part of our shaping is taking in aspects that come from others. These can be our families, cultures, religions, social media, peers, celebrities, teachers, professors, administration, and so forth. ALL of these can impact our viewpoints, which directly affects our teaching. These can often unintentionally cause biases that we may have of others. Part of this self-reflection process is beginning to locate these biases so we can help navigate and incorporate more inclusive best practices.

WHAT IS THE PURPOSE OF THIS TEXT?

As we begin to explore accessible strategies for teaching music, we need to consider where the field of music education currently stands. There is currently much discussion about equity in music education happening at the national, state, and local levels. This is great, as we need to have these discussions to analyze our profession and ensure that everyone can make music in a way that works for and connects to them. This includes our students and our fellow music educators.

Because I primarily teach in a center-based special education program, most of the students I teach are students with disabilities. The core focus of this book is teaching students who learn, engage, and make music in different ways. Nevertheless, we must highlight the gaps in our teacher training programs. Many college programs do not offer coursework in teaching music to students with disabilities. Some colleges may have a general course on students with disabilities, but it is not content specific to music. Other programs try to infuse this topic into other methods classes. However, it is not enough.

I am not mentioning this to insult the excellent teacher preparation programs that exist. I understand that college programs face obstacles when trying to meet these needs. Nevertheless, by not preparing music educators to teach a wide range of learners, we are not giving our future teachers the tools to engage ALL students. Our students are not receiving a meaningful, individualized music education that works for them.

In a 2023 *PBS NewsHour* special on the Berklee Institute of Accessible Arts Education (BIAAE), Jeffrey Brown interviewed founding director Dr. Rhoda Bernard, who perfectly mentions that "arts educators are generally trained to teach the way they were taught. There are long-standing traditions in how the arts have been taught." She then mentions "like the conservatory tradition of what a private lesson looks like. Often, the arts can be more of a teacher-centered kind of approach, where the teacher is showing what they want, and the students are responding."[1]

We are not taught to teach in a way that reaches every student, and this is a problem. The connection gap between students and teachers is drastically moving further apart. The COVID-19 pandemic further exposed and increased the cracks in our education system. The system has never worked for ALL, and we need to pause and reset how we can move forward from here.

Although many fantastic resources and texts exist regarding teaching music to students with disabilities (many will be cited throughout this book), we must also take this information and consider *how* to implement it. My aim and focus in this text is to use ALL of our previous resources and put them in a practical lens of what it looks like using musical examples. I recognize that some of you may be seasoned teachers whereas others are in teacher preparation programs. I will write this text to focus on everyone in ALL aspects of their careers.

This text will serve as a continuum to the amazing work already done. Overall, we need to alter and update our teaching approach to ensure that we teach in a way that reaches ALL. In this time of increasing teacher shortages in our field, ALL teachers must have the tools to engage every student.

ACCESS VERSUS BARRIERS

One of the words used repeatedly throughout this text is **access**. Consider, do ALL students have access to participate in our music programs? Do ALL students have access to participate in festivals and adjudications?

Do ALL students have access to engage with musical learning? Do music educators have access to the tools and resources to create a meaningful musical experience for ALL?

These guiding questions will be answered and highlighted in our journey. Another word that easily connects to the word access is **inclusion**. The definition of inclusion according to 42 U.S. Code § 15002 (15) highlights "the acceptance and encouragement of the presence and participation of individuals with developmental disabilities, by individuals without disabilities, in social, educational, work, and community activities, that enables individuals with developmental disabilities."[2]

When we consider the definition of inclusion, we think about a classroom that may have students without disabilities combined with students who have disabilities. This is inaccurate. Instead, consider inclusion as everyone in that one classroom having access to learn in a way that works for them and gives them a feeling of belonging.

We also need to consider the opposite of access, which is **barriers**. A connecting word to this would be **exclusion**. What are the barriers to the musical content that we teach? Which students are excluded from our music programs? Which students are excluded from the content that we teach? Which students are excluded from our festivals and adjudications? Unfortunately, this is the world we live in, where many students are excluded for various reasons. Even more, many barriers exist in our content and field, further enhancing a sense of exclusion.

I aim to empower you with the tools and strategies to ensure that ALL students feel a sense of **belonging**. We strive to foster an environment where ALL students feel **welcome**. It is not just about recognizing that every one of our students is different. We need to consider many aspects in our classrooms and ensembles that allow our students to have a sense of belonging.

In her book *UNMASKED*, activist Ellie Middleton mentions that "we've never actually taken a minute to stop and consider whether the education system works for everybody, the workplace works for everybody or society in general works for everybody—and that has meant that, for a lot of us, it doesn't."[3] In their book *Say the Right Thing*, Meltzer Center for Diversity, Inclusion, and Belonging directors Kenji Yoshino, and David Glasgow mention that "it's to hear those who speak of the inequalities in our world, and to raise our voices as allies in support of their quest for justice. It's to say the right thing, not in the sense of obeying rules of etiquette, but in the sense of speaking up for what's right."[4]

We need to do better. We have the tools to give everyone a sense of belonging and welcome. Let us work together to re-create a musical field where everyone has access to make music in a way that works for them, not just for us.

ALL

The other word I want to highlight is **ALL**. The strategies, concepts, and ideas we will discuss are primarily designed for students with disabilities or the most needs. Nevertheless, these strategies benefit ALL. And that is the focus of this work. As teachers, we cannot wait until we hear that a student needs changes in their environment and only make them during that time. We need to change our teaching approach and teach in a way that meets ALL learners regularly. This is only good teaching.

During a 2022 ABLE Conversation with the Berklee Institute of Accessible Arts Education (BIAAE) presented by Rebecca Cokley from the Ford Foundation, she shared an image titled *Inequality, Equality, Equity, and Justice* from Boston University's Diversity & Inclusion web page (Boston University, n.d.). The image describes four boxes of people viewing a baseball game with a fence blocking the game titled reality, equality, equity, and justice. In reality, the taller person has multiple boxes to stand on to view the game, whereas the shorter person gets nothing. In education, this connects to some students having access, opportunities, or resources whereas others have none.

In the equality box, everyone gets the same. But as you can see, this still does not benefit ALL or give everyone the same access. Since one person is taller, that person still has a clear view of the game. The shorter person still cannot view the game, even with a box. In our schools, giving everyone the same resources does not mean that it works for ALL.

In the equity box, each person gets what they need to view the game. The taller person does not need a box, so they can stand and view the game without one. The shorter person gets the number of boxes they need to view the game. In education, every student receives the support they need to be successful. This sounds like the ideal situation, correct?

But we have one final box—justice. What if the fence was never there in the first place? This brings us back to the word "barriers." The fence is the barrier; if we remove it, everyone benefits. This is the angle of this text. ALL benefit when the barrier is removed.

HOW TO USE THIS TEXT

The strategies we will discuss are current educational trends and techniques that can be applied immediately in your classroom. It is evidence-based classroom practice and as a practical resource, it is intentionally designed to support you in creating an accessible environment for your students. The definitions I provide are not just my own but tailored to break down complex concepts practically. Rest assured; resources will be provided throughout this book to further your journey in creating an accessible music classroom.

As mentioned, I primarily teach in a center-based special education program. Although we discuss strategies and techniques, I will provide examples of these in action. It is important to note that the examples I will showcase are not the only way this looks but ways that work for my students and my teaching style. They can be modified to suit your students and your teaching style.

It will look different for you. Your students, their needs, your community, and you are different. While we go through these examples, reflect on what these would look like for you. I already can acknowledge where gaps in this text may arise. These strategies are transferable to ALL ages and ALL types of music. Again, reflect on what these would look like for you.

If there are any inaccuracies throughout this text, they are not intentional, and I apologize for them now. I am a human being, and I am on my own pathway of unlearning and growth. I am writing this to support you with the knowledge and experience I have gained. In time, some of these ideas may need to be updated. This is what happens in the field of education, as it is constantly updated.

So, buckle up, and here we go. Let us begin to make *The Music Classroom Accessible to ALL*.

NOTES

1. Jeffrey Brown, Anne A. Davenport, and Alison Thoet, "How an Elite Music School Is Increasing Access for Students with Disabilities," *PBS NewsHour*, September 7, 2023, https://www.pbs.org/newshour/show/how-an-elite-music-school-is-increasing-access-for-students-with-disabilities.

2. "42 U.S. Code § 15002–Definitions," LII/Legal Information Institute, Cornell Law School, accessed August 25, 2024, https://www.law.cornell.edu/uscode/text/42/15002#15.

3. Ellie Middleton, *UNMASKED: The Ultimate Guide to ADHD, Autism and Neurodivergence* (Random House, 2023), 238.

4. Kenji Yoshino and David Glasgow, *Say the Right Thing: How to Talk about Identity, Diversity, and Justice* (Simon & Schuster, 2023), 14.

Chapter 2

Who Is ALL?

ESSENTIAL QUESTIONS

1. Who are the students in our music classrooms and ensembles?
2. What is neurodiversity, and why is a strength-based approach beneficial for ALL students?

CORE VOCABULARY

Neurodiversity, neurotypical, neurodivergence, neurodivergent, engage, strength-based model, disabilities, visible disabilities, non-apparent disabilities, invisible disabilities, hidden disabilities, masking, thirteen disability categories, higher support needs, *Diagnostic and Statistical Manual of Mental Disorders (DSM-V)*, Individuals with Disabilities Education Act (IDEA), special education services and programs, zero reject, nondiscriminatory evaluation, free and appropriate education (FAPE), least restrictive environment (LRE), procedural due process, parent involvement, Americans with Disabilities Act (ADA), Every Student Succeeds Act (ESSA), individualized education program (IEP), related services, 504 accommodation plan, behavioral intervention plan (BIP), formal behavioral analysis (FBA), gifted and talented, twice exceptional (2E), English learners (EL), LGBTQIA2S+ community, intersectionality

OPENING THOUGHTS: WHO ARE OUR STUDENTS?

Welcome to the first day of school: there is no energy like the start of a new year. Imagine that you have spent the past week setting up your music classroom for success. This week, you get your student roster, including student names and background information. The first day goes by like a whirlwind, and now you have time to reflect. Close your eyes, think about the musical environment you have set up, and think about the students you have taught—and whether your roster or information accurately describes your students.

Think about these four questions:

1. What do you see in your classroom music environment (suggested ideas: musical instruments, desks, risers, posters and charts, student work, laptops or computers, a colorful rug, a cart filled with musical materials, chairs, etc.)?
2. Who are the students? Think about many ways that each of your students may be slightly different. How many differences do you come up with? Can you define each one clearly? Did the background information you received accurately describe them?
3. Think about yourself now as the teacher. What are some challenges you feel knowing that there is an array of differences between your students? Do you feel prepared to teach ALL of them? How do you think your students feel?
4. What are the benefits of having a wide range of learners in your classroom? What do you think your students are learning from each other? What are you learning from them? How does it impact making music in your classroom?

Most likely, some of your answers to the third question would be in line with not being able to reach every student, feeling overwhelmed with creating differentiation, feeling a lack of preparation, and feeling a lack of understanding of some students' backgrounds. If these were some of your thoughts—do not be alarmed. Most of us have felt the same way when we are teaching and trying to engage ALL students.

So, how do we make it work? Is it possible to reach ALL students, especially in a classroom with a wide range of learning styles? Absolutely!

Yes, we definitely have work to do. Nevertheless, when we are ready to reflect on our teaching practice and be willing to unlearn ideas that may not be fully inclusive, we then can create a music classroom accessible to ALL!

MUSIC FOR ALL

As music teachers, we often find ourselves in teaching situations where we teach ALL. This means that, in some instances, we may teach every student within a campus (or even multiple campuses). In other instances, we may teach students in cohorts, semesters, different grades, electives, and clubs randomly. Nevertheless, even if we just take one class of twenty-five students, that class alone has a wide range of learning styles.

However, who is considered ALL? Included may be students who

- are neurotypical;
- are neurodivergent;
- have disabilities (both visible and non-apparent);
- who receive special education services and programs;
- who have higher support needs;
- who need support in different areas or domains;
- who have trauma or need support with mental health;
- who are gifted and talented;
- who are twice exceptional (2E);
- who are English learners (EL);
- who are part of the LGBTQIA2S+ community; and
- who may be in temporary housing or are homeless.

More categories definitely can be included. Nevertheless, this may be a realistic image of who is in our classrooms or ensembles. I mention this list not to stress you out but to add context to the word ALL. As music teachers, *we teach ALL!*

Knowing that you must prepare a lesson that engages such a range of learners can seem overwhelming, impossible, daunting, or unrealistic. As you probably answered in the question above, in one class period alone, you may have a vast span of different ways that students learn, process, and ultimately make music. You may also wonder how it is humanly possible to reach every student without making your head explode. That is where the rest of this resourceful book comes in. It does involve work on our part, but it is worth it. Wouldn't it be amazing for ALL students to have a place to make music in a way that works for them?

It is essential to highlight that as we mention context to the word ALL, at the end of the day, ALL students are human beings first. We are ALL part of the same genus and species. ALL humans have basic wants, needs, strengths, and interests. Although ALL our students need food, shelter, and care, they also have unique interests and aspects that they can bring to the classroom. For example, many of our students are avid video game players, which can easily connect to musical and repertoire selection (or even incorporating technology such as a Makey Makey). ALL our students are capable of amazing things, and it is up to us as teachers to recognize them as human beings first and create an environment shaped around their strengths and interests.

As we explore who our students are and add up-to-date language and terminology, something is extraordinary about the fact that we can reach ALL. Not every teacher in our students' lives can reach such a broad audience of learners and can impact positive change in so many ways. Most importantly, one thing that we will begin to explore later is that the strategies designed for some will benefit ALL.

THE NEURODIVERSE MUSIC CLASSROOM

Now that we have added context to many of the students we teach, what word can we use to describe the vast differences between their learning styles? That word would be **neurodiversity**. If we take apart the word, we get *neuro* (brain) and *diversity* (differences).

Australian sociologist Judy Singer, considered the mother of neurodiversity, coined the term in her honors thesis in 1998. In her introduction, she mentions that "as new identities, alliances, and movements form and re-form themselves, there are signs everywhere that we are beginning to divide ourselves not only along the familiar lines of ethnicity, class, gender, and disability, but according to something new: differences in 'kinds of minds.'"[1]

Singer felt that a description of how our brains operate differently was needed, which was the birth of neurodiversity. Neurodiversity is simply that each of our brains works in its own way—how we learn, experience the world around us, process and decode new information, complete a task, and so forth. Some people experience the world more similarly to each other, which we call **neurotypical**. Other people and brains experience the world differently, which is called **neurodivergence**. People who experience neurodivergence are **neurodivergent**. Some common examples of neurodivergence include people with ADHD, autism, dyslexia, and more.

Nevertheless, we need to emphasize that we are talking about human beings. Our entire world is neurodiverse because we are ALL vastly different. When we use the label neurotypical, even this can be broken down in many ways. I believe that we are ALL neurodivergent to an extent. Human beings do not fall into categories where we are either *this* or *that* or can be categorized in columns on a T-chart. We ALL have strengths in some areas and are ALL challenged by others. We must be cautious and mindful of our language when referring to human beings. I cringe when I hear words such as *normal, regular ed,* or *high functioning*. We are ALL just people experiencing life in the way our brains and bodies were created.

So, what does neurodiversity have to do in our music classrooms? We need to be aware that every student will learn in their own unique way. Every student will also **engage** in their own way. For the rest of this book, I will connect the word *engage* to the National Core Arts Standards' four artistic processes (create, perform, respond, and connect).[2] To restate this critical point: each student will musically engage (create, perform, respond, and connect) in their own unique way—and that is OK. There is no consensus on what the ideal model student should be. We are ALL vastly different, so let us create a world that celebrates this.

In his book *Neurodiversity in the Classroom*, iconic educator Thomas Armstrong mentions that teachers should focus on what our students *can* do, not what they *can't*. His approach is one of many examples of the strength-based model. **ALL students can!** He mentions that "instead of regarding these students as suffering from deficit, disease, or dysfunction, neurodiversity suggests that we speak about their *strengths*."[3]

Rather than having ALL students conform to our standards and expectations, we should shape the environment around their individual needs and strengths. This means that we need to be aware of the potential barriers in our physical environment, curriculum, learning objectives, repertoire selection, and performance expectations. We need to shape our content around the needs and strengths of our students.

Music educators should be mindful that this does not just apply to students who have the most needs or legal documentation that requires adaptations in the classroom. We need to recognize our students' strengths and shape a learning experience around them, rather than forcing them to conform to our expectations of what we want the *norm* to be.

STUDENTS WITH DISABILITIES

In our music classrooms and ensembles, we have students who have **disabilities**. According to the Centers for Disease Control and Prevention (CDC), "a disability is any condition of the body or mind (impairment) that makes it more difficult for the person with the condition to do certain activities (activity limitation) and interact with the world around them (participation restrictions)."[4] According to a 2023 statistic, about 7.3 million students in public schools had a disability during the 2021–2022 school year—which equates to about 15 percent of the student population.[5] The CDC's most current statistic is that 27 percent (one in four adults) have some type of disability.[6]

The word "disability" is not a bad word, but unfortunately, our culture has treated it as such. Individuals with disabilities are entirely able to achieve remarkable outcomes. It is the world around them and the actions of nondisabled people that create the barriers that restrict them from accessing aspects that can showcase their true potential.

Music teachers should be aware that the idea of having a disability can vary for different families or communities. Music teachers can support ALL and focus on each student's strengths. Be mindful that families might be going through their own stages of acceptance. In some instances, a stigma may be attached to having a disability. This can resonate very differently for each situation. Our job is not to judge but to be an ally and advocate for every student.

Disabilities can be divided into two categories: Some students will have **visible disabilities**—disabilities that we can observe. For example, a student may use crutches, a wheelchair, or a communication device, require cochlear implants or a hearing aid, or use prosthetic limbs. Even more, many students may have legal documentation that teachers are aware of and legally mandated to follow.

Other students may have **non-apparent disabilities**. Sometimes you may hear these referred to as **invisible disabilities** or **hidden disabilities**. Be aware that these two terms have very different meanings. A student with a non-apparent disability may not have any legal documentation or diagnosis. Some students and families may be unaware or choose not to disclose it for various reasons. Some examples of individuals with non-apparent disabilities may include mental health, chronic illness, physical or medical disabilities, learning differences, and autism.

Some students may have gotten so used to hiding their disability that this is called **masking**. Ellie Middleton says, "put simply, masking is when an autistic (or otherwise neurodivergent) person attempts to appear non-autistic (or neurotypical) by covering up their autistic (or neurodivergent) traits."[7] A student who is masking may be using ALL their energy to try to conform to a neurotypical world rather than the world being shaped around their individual needs and strengths.

Music teachers should be aware that more individuals have non-apparent disabilities than with visible ones. Teachers should not wait for a student to have a formal diagnosis or documentation. Instead, they should teach and engage ALL students in a way that reaches every student consistently. More to come on this later.

Anyone can have a disability. Some disabilities can be temporary, and others can be permanent. For example, some students might be fine one day and then come in the next with a cast on their arm from doing something silly. Others may be born with a disability or may acquire it at some point during their life. Nevertheless, we need to focus on their abilities, not their deficits. As we have mentioned already, every one of our students can—and that should be our focus.

Per the Individuals with Disabilities Education Act Section 300.8 (IDEA), **thirteen disability categories** are listed by the United States Department of Education.[8] These include

- autism (ASD)
- deafness

- deaf-blindness
- emotional disturbance
- hearing impairment
- intellectual disability
- multiple disabilities
- orthopedic impairment
- other heath-impairment
- specific learning disabilities (SLD)
- speech or language impairment
- traumatic brain injury
- visual impairment

These classifications, or labels, are used so students can receive the appropriate support and funding for their individualized programs. *This label does not define the student.* Every one of our students can achieve amazing things when the environment is shaped around their strengths. Different states may have modified or even added to this list. For example, New Jersey has added a category for ALL preschool-age children. In addition, some states have already, or are in the process of, updating some of the language (e.g., emotional disturbance is an out-of-date term).

Students within each category have a wide range of strengths and differences. Do not assume that every student with the same classification will be the same. Remember, every student is a unique being.

Some students may have **higher support needs**. Let us get out of the habit of using the term *low functioning*. Again, we are talking about humans. Some students just need more help or support to achieve their best. These can include students who are nonspeakers (students who may use augmentative and alternative communication, or AAC), students who are highly hypersensitive or hyposensitive to the environment around them, students who may require hand-over-hand assistive or prompting when asked, or students who may have limited ambulatory access to making music.

Let us focus on what our students CAN do and their endless array of possibilities. Amazing things will happen when our students' strengths are supported and incorporated.

Note: teachers are not medical professionals. Teachers cannot diagnose a student with a disability; only someone within the medical field can.

Medical personnel typically use the **Diagnostic and Statistical Manual of Mental Disorders (DSM-V)** to formally evaluate and diagnose a student. If you suspect a student may need more support, work with the school community and special education team to evaluate the appropriate protocol with your district and state regulations.

FEDERAL LAWS

Music teachers must be aware of several groundbreaking federal laws protecting ALL students and their families. These laws help impact funding that goes to schools and districts to support students, which services a student might be eligible for and how to receive them, civil rights protections, accessible elements to ALL locations, and direct teaching practices and strategies that will be directly implemented in the classroom. These laws apply to ALL classroom settings, including the music classroom and ensembles.

The Office of Special Education and Rehabilitative Services through the U.S. Department of Education[9] offers many resources teachers should know about. Music teachers should also be familiar with their own state's laws and regulations, as they may differ slightly from state to state. Each state should have up-to-date rules and regulations on its education website.

The **Individuals with Disabilities Education Act (IDEA)**[10] is a law that originated from Public Law 94-142. This law requires ALL school districts to identify, locate, and evaluate ALL children with disabilities ages 0–21 at no cost to the parent/guardian. This law applies to public or private schools, as well as home-based programs. Some states have recently begun to modify the maximum age to twenty-two due to the loss of instruction and mandated related services due to the COVID-19 pandemic. Some students may require **special education services and programs**, as the general education curriculum may not meet their individualized needs. These programs are specially and individually designed as every student's needs differ.

There are six principles of IDEA:

1. **Zero reject** states that no student can be excluded from any type of classroom or setting due to having a disability. ALL students have the

right to an education, and ALL means ALL. For music teachers, no student can be denied access to music education or participation in an ensemble due to a disability.
2. A team will evaluate a student through a **nondiscriminatory evaluation**. This team will discuss appropriate placement, strategies, supports, goals, and services for the student. Parents and guardians are part of this team, along with staff members at the school or program.
3. Every student is entitled to a **free, appropriate public education (FAPE)**. The team will decide what type of classroom setting, program, and services will best support a student.
4. Students will be placed in a **least restrictive environment (LRE)** or in an environment where students thrive best. Students with disabilities will be educated with students without disabilities for the maximum amount of time possible. For example, some students may do well in a general education classroom. Others may strive in an integrated co-taught classroom (ICT), self-contained classroom, or a center-based special education program. A student's LRE can change over time.
5. ALL families and guardians have legal rights through **procedural due process**. Parents and guardians have the right to request a change in placement, and the team will reconvene to discuss appropriate support.
6. **Parent involvement** is essential for every student. Parents and guardians are integral to each student's success. Schools should also provide additional support to help families at home.

The **Americans with Disabilities Act of 1990 (ADA)**[11] is a landmark civil rights law prohibiting any discrimination of individuals with disabilities in any public location. This includes schools, the community, transportation, housing, medical, and government centers. Through this law, music teachers must be aware of any support or needs that a student may require. Music teachers should ensure that their classrooms, performance spaces, and performances are accessible to ALL. Music teachers should also consider music-making activities outside the school building or day, such as field trips, festivals, or adjudications.

Every Student Succeeds Act of 2015 (ESSA)[12] is the most current law, preceded by No Child Left Behind (NCLB) and the Elementary and Secondary Act (ESEA). The focus of this law is that every student is designed a pathway for success. Music is included in the language of this law as part of a well-rounded education. For music teachers, this includes access to the general education curriculum, access to accommodations on assessments, universal design for learning (UDL), and incorporating evidence-based strategies.

LEGAL DOCUMENTATION

Along with federal laws and regulations, music teachers must also be aware of the legal documentation many students may have. In addition, if a student has any of the documents below in their records, then ALL teachers (including music and specialty teachers) are legally responsible for reading them and incorporating any strategies or supports listed.

The primary type of documentation that a student may have listed is an **individualized education program (IEP)**. The IEP is a legal document annually reviewed by a team of professionals and family members. The purpose of this document is for the team to decide which adaptations, accommodations, or modifications may be necessary for the student and which **related services** are necessary (e.g., speech and language, occupational therapy, physical therapy, counseling, hearing or vision services, feeding therapy, music or art therapy); and what the least restrictive environment should be. The IEP will contain a student profile sheet; current levels of functioning; measurable and achievable goals in areas such as reading, writing, and math; information about the student such as behavioral supports, management needs, physical development, supports that need to be provided, related service goals, transportation needs, and transition plans.

Music teachers are legally responsible for reading this document for each student at the beginning of the school year. Music teachers are also responsible for incorporating the listed strategies and needs, as this document is legally binding. Although this may sound overwhelming, because teachers may have many students with plans that recommend individualized strategies and supports, many of these can be incorporated into daily routines regularly and benefit ALL students.

Music teachers should also note the privacy aspect of an IEP. Only teachers and staff directly teaching the student will have access to the IEP. The information cannot be shared with outside members who serve the child due to student privacy law, Family Educational Rights and Privacy Act (FERPA). In addition, music teachers should note that they can be asked to attend an IEP meeting when it happens. However, music teachers should not be writing an IEP unless they have multiple licenses and are working under a special education license. Nevertheless, music teachers can recommend that students' musical strengths and interests be added to the IEP.

Other students may have a **504 Accommodation Plan**. These plans are designed to assist students to engage with their general education peers at an equal level. In another sense, these general adaptations allow them equal access in the general education classroom. You may sometimes hear that a 504 Accommodation Plan is designed to *level the playing field*. Although an IEP can last an entire student's academic career, a 504 Accommodation Plan can sometimes be temporary. Some common examples include extended test time, using specific materials such as a calculator, and using an elevator rather than stairs.

Some students may have a **behavioral intervention plan (BIP)**. This specific behavior plan is typically an amendment within an IEP. Therefore, a BIP is also a legal document. A team will complete a BIP using a **formal behavioral analysis (FBA)**. Once a specific behavior is targeted, a plan is implemented to help support the student. Data is collected regularly to ensure that the plan in place is working. We will discuss behaviors in more detail later in this book.

SIX DOMAINS

As mentioned, not every student may have a formal diagnosis or classified disability. Moreover, some students may just need support in various areas that may not require a formal intervention. Music teachers should be aware of the different types of support some students may need. They should also consider how music can help support these areas and how their teaching approach can make aspects more successful.

In their book *Teaching Music to Students with Special Needs*, Alice Hammel and Ryan Hourigan mention six domains, rather than focusing on the specific disabilities of students. These domains include behavioral, cognition, communication, emotional, physical, and sensory. They write, "focusing on these challenges may allow music teachers to simplify their instructional strategies and deliver higher quality instruction to students. In addition, this approach allows music teachers to focus on the whole person instead of the disability that challenges the student."[13]

Although there is much overlap between these six domains, I recommend an extra focus on mental health. Knowing where our students are currently after the disruption in their education during the COVID-19 pandemic, I personally believe that we should consider the mental health of ALL students as well and recognize any trauma that they have gone through in their lives. We will connect to the six domains later in the book.

MORE INCLUDED IN ALL

Music teachers will have additional students in their classrooms and ensembles with their own needs. For example, some students may be **gifted and talented**. These are students who have demonstrated high achievement in specific academic areas. Music and the arts can be some of these areas. Many students may be naturally gifted at music and can engage and perform at a more advanced level than others. Some schools or programs may have a designated gifted and talented program or class, whereas in other instances, the students may be included in a general education classroom. The Jacob K. Javits Gifted and Talented Students Education Program[14] helps support gifted and talented programs within schools through grants, research, and assistance.

Some students may be **twice exceptional (2E)**. A student who is 2E may be gifted in some aspects but may also have a disability. For example, a student may be classified as gifted and talented but may require a 504 Accommodation Plan for a medical or physical reason. This can also happen the other way: for example, a student who may be in a self-contained classroom for either academic or social support may be highly gifted at music.

Other students may be **English learners (EL)**.[15] You may alternately hear the terminology ELL (English language learner) or ENL (English as a new language). EL is the current terminology used by the U.S. Department of Education. Some students may speak more than one language. They may be bilingual or even trilingual. EL services are provided for the students who require them. According to the U.S. Department of Education, 10 percent of students were EL during the 2014–2015 school year (U.S. Department of Education, n.d.).

Some students may be part of the **LGBTQIA2S+ community** (lesbian, gay, bisexual, transgender, questioning, intersex, asexual, and two-spirit). Some may identify or refer to their sexual orientation, some through their gender identity, whereas others may be transgender or nonbinary. Music teachers must ensure that the music classroom and ensemble are safe spaces for ALL. Music teachers must also be aware that some students may not get the support they need at home.

Some students may live in temporary housing, be homeless, or be in foster care. These situations can be due to various factors at home that are out of their control. Music teachers need to create a safe space where students feel comfortable, have their basic needs met, and where they can feel a sense of belonging.

Lastly, music teachers need to be aware of the **intersectionality** of ALL. The term intersectionality was coined by law professor Kimberlé Crenshaw in 1989. In their book *Intersectionality*, sociology professors Patricia Hill Collins and Sirma Bilge write, "as an analytic tool, intersectionality views categories of race, class, gender, sexuality, nation, ability, ethnicity, and age—among others—as interrelated and mutually shaping one another. Intersectionality is a way of understanding and explaining complexity in the world, in people, and in human experiences."[16]

Music teachers need to recognize the many intersections that our students have and how they may impact their academic and social career at school. Many students may have multiple intersections that create additional barriers that may not exist for others. For example, a student may be BIPOC (black, indigenous, and people of color), part of the LGBTQIA2S+ community, and have a disability as well. Because students from marginalized communities often face increased barriers or discrimination in education, music teachers also need to be receptive to what they are teaching, how they are teaching, and what they are using to teach. Empathy, understanding, and willingness to see from our students' perspectives are the best ways to help create a welcoming environment for ALL.

CLOSING COMMENTS

At the beginning of this chapter, we did an activity where we reflected on who the different students in our classrooms are. We considered the various types of learners in one classroom setting, let alone our programs or school. We then reflected that as music teachers, we often teach ALL students. We then spent the rest of the chapter defining who many of the students are in our classrooms and adding up-to-date terminology and language.

Although this should be familiar to many of you, some parts may be new, which is OK. As teachers, we are lifelong learners ourselves. In addition, we need to recognize that the landscape will constantly change and shift, and with that, language and terminology will be updated. We must stay current with educational and political trends, as they are how we can best support ALL students in reaching their full potential.

If this chapter felt like it covered too much in too short of space, the American Psychological Association has created a bias-free language resource on its website.[17] Although this is used primarily for academic writing and research, it can easily be used as a tool for teachers in how we speak about our students. We will discuss more about language use in the next chapter.

REFLECTION QUESTIONS

1. Why is a strength-based model important, and how do you currently incorporate your students' strengths in the classroom? How would you do so, if not so already?
2. Why do you think it is important to consider students with non-apparent disabilities instead of waiting for formal documentation or a diagnosis?

3. Why can't a music teacher contact a family or guardian member to suggest or diagnose that a student may have a disability?
4. Why is it important to consider the student as a whole person first rather than just focusing on their disability or classification?

NOTES

1. Judy Singer, *Neurodiversity: The Birth of an Idea* ([AU]2017), 27.

2. "What Are the National Arts Standards?," National Core Arts Standards, accessed August 25, 2024, https://www.nationalartsstandards.org/.

3. Thomas Armstrong, *Neurodiversity in the Classroom: Strength-Based Strategies to Help Students with Special Needs Succeed in School and Life* (ASCD, 2012), 9.

4. "Disability and Health Overview," Disability and Health Promotion, CDC, last modified April 3, 2024, https://www.cdc.gov/ncbddd/disabilityandhealth/disability.html.

5. Katherine Schaeffer, "What Federal Education Data Shows about Students with Disabilities in the U.S.," *Pew Research Center*, April 14, 2024, https://www.pewresearch.org/short-reads/2023/07/24/what-federal-education-data-shows-about-students-with-disabilities-in-the-us/#:~:text=The%207.3%20million%20disabled%20students,the%202021%2D22%20school%20year.

6. "Disability Impacts All of Us," Disability and Health Promotion, CDC, last modified July 3, 2024, https://www.cdc.gov/ncbddd/disabilityandhealth/infographic-disability-impacts-all.html.

7. Ellie Middleton, *UNMASKED: The Ultimate Guide to ADHD, Autism and Neurodivergence* (Random House, 2023), 155.

8. "Statute and Regulations," Individuals with Disabilities Education Act, accessed August 25, 2024, https://sites.ed.gov/idea/statuteregulations/.

9. "Office of Special Education and Rehabilitative Services," OSERS, U.S. Department of Education, last modified April 4, 2023, https://www2.ed.gov/about/offices/list/osers/osep/index.html.

10. Individuals with Disabilities Education Act, "Statute and Regulations."

11. "The Americans with Disabilities Act (ADA) protects people with disabilities from discrimination," U.S. Department of Justice Civil Rights Division, ADA, accessed August 25, 2024, https://www.ada.gov/.

12. "Every Student Succeeds Act (ESSA)," U.S. Department of Education, accessed August 25, 2024, https://www.ed.gov/essa?src=ft.

13. Alice M. Hammel and Ryan M. Hourigan, *Teaching Music to Students with Special Needs: A Label-Free Approach*, second edition (Oxford University Press, 2017), 13.

14. "Jacob K. Javits Gifted and Talented Students Education Program," Office of Elementary and Secondary Education, last modified February 6, 2024, https://oese.ed.gov/offices/office-of-discretionary-grants-support-services/well-rounded-education-programs/jacob-k-javits-gifted-and-talented-students-education-program/.

15. "Our Nation's English Learners," U.S. Department of Education, accessed August 25, 2024, https://www2.ed.gov/datastory/el-characteristics/index.html.

16. Patricia H. Collins and Sirma Bilge, *Intersectionality*, second edition (Polity Press, 2020), 2.

17. "Bias-Free Language," APA Style, American Psychological Association, last modified November 2023, https://apastyle.apa.org/style-grammar-guidelines/bias-free-language.

Chapter 3

Who Shapes the Strength-Based Environment?

ESSENTIAL QUESTIONS

1. How can music educators be aware of how they view or describe their students, what biases they have, and how these impact the music classroom?
2. How can music educators consider their students' strengths, and what does the strength-based model look like?

CORE VOCABULARY

High-quality music education, standards-based music education, key players, classroom teachers, special education teachers, administrators, related service providers, paraprofessionals, teaching assistants, families and community members, outside organizations and resources, unlearning, unintentional barriers, medical model, charity model, social model, neurodiversity affirming model, language, person-first language (PFL), identity-first language (IFL), ableism, ableist, bias, implicit bias, strength-based model, positive niche construction, developing independence, student empowerment, voice and choice, solid teamwork, belief that ALL can

OPENING THOUGHTS: VIGNETTE

It is halfway through the school year, and Ms. Greer has been delving deep into her music curriculum with her middle-school students. She has just been informed that a new student (Adrian) will join one of her classes the following week, as he has just moved. Adrian has a diagnosis of autism and has an IEP. Adrian also has a 1:1 crisis paraprofessional assigned to him. During the school day, he is in a self-contained special education classroom; however, Adrian's class will be combined with a general education class during music and specialty periods. Ms. Greer looks at her schedule and sees that his assigned class has music the following Friday.

Throughout the week, she reads through his IEP, as she wants to make sure that she is prepared to support him. Nevertheless, over the next few days, talk about "the new boy" comes through other staff. In the staff lounge, Ms. Greer overhears other teachers making comments such as "he is difficult," "he is nonverbal," "why is he in my class?," "he is unlearnable." She starts to wonder about Adrian and begins to doubt his skills before music on Friday.

On Friday, the class arrives with Adrian and his paraprofessional. The paraprofessional pulls Ms. Greer aside beforehand and says, "Good luck; he should not even be allowed to come to music." Throughout the music class, Adrian runs around the room, yells, grabs materials and items from the shelves, and will not let anyone near him. Ms. Greer can tell that the other students are confused; some may even be frustrated that the class needs to stop multiple times. By the end of the class, she feels defeated and discouraged. She is ready to consider speaking to her administrator about possibly removing Adrian from music class.

Think about the following:

1. Should Adrian be taken out of music? Why or why not (hint: think back to the previous chapter)?
2. What impact did the discussions overheard throughout the week have on the music teacher in this situation? Did it impact Ms. Greer's opinion of Adrian?
3. How do you think the colleagues outside the music classroom feel about Adrian? How do you think this will impact Adrian's success at school?
4. What can Ms. Greer do in this situation?

This situation can happen in any type of music program. In this example, yes, Adrian sounds like he has higher support needs to be met. Yet, remember—he is still a human being with basic wants, needs, strengths, and interests. For most teachers, the first day of having a new student in class is more about observation and getting to know each other. A successful plan will likely not happen on day one—and that is OK. An accessible music classroom takes time and practice, and there are multiple types of applications; sometimes, there is a failure to reflect on the next steps.

Should Adrian be removed from the music room? The answer is no. He has a legal right to be there; removing him should not be considered. However, once the music teacher gets to know Adrian better, they can work with the paraprofessional and special education team to develop appropriate strategies to support him.

When Ms. Greer overheard colleagues talking about Adrian, that did not help. In this situation, she may already have developed an unintentional bias before meeting Adrian. This bias may have impacted how she now feels about Adrian's ability to participate in music class.

In this example, the staff outside the music classroom have already developed a bias against Adrian. Our role is to be an ally and support for every student. Once plans are implemented, we can create an environment where Adrian can succeed. Lastly, what can Ms. Greer do? Check out the next few chapters as we dive into making it an accessible classroom for Adrian and his peers.

WHY MUSIC?

If someone were to ask you why you do what you do, how would you answer this? Even more, can you answer why you teach music and what music means to you? Although these are two simple questions, they both require thought. We may teach because we had inspiring music teachers ourselves, want to use the arts to reach the whole child, build vital performance-based programs, or give musical options where previously access may have been limited. These are valid and great answers.

For me, it ALL comes back to music. Music has always meant more to me than anything else in the world. Whether it is through listening, performing, teaching, or even creating—music is the core of who I am as a human being. I also had inspiring music teachers growing up. They helped infuse musical identity within me, and I now want to pass the same opportunity to the next generation of students.

When I decided to become a music teacher, this was the legacy that I wanted to pass along to others. How can my students use music to find who they are, how they identify, and how can music positively impact them outside school? I am fortunate enough to teach in a program where I have seen a positive impact directly on my students.

Fast-forward years later, and I have seen how music reaches more than into the soul of every student. In a 2008 interview with *Brain and Life Magazine*, Andrea Cooper interviewed neurologist Oliver Sacks, who said that "music doesn't convey information in the usual sense; it doesn't represent anything in the external world, but it can move one to the depths. Music has the power to elicit every emotion, and every mood, and every state of mind there is. I think this is why it exists in every culture."[1] In addition, in her book *Including Everyone*, Judith A. Jellison, professor emeritus at the University of Texas at Austin, says that "the long-term goal for all students is to experience meaningful music participation throughout life, alone and with others in their schools, homes, and communities."[2]

The benefits of music and music education being a necessity for ALL are endless. Music reaches every student academically, emotionally, socially, personally, culturally, intrinsically, and more. Music brings joy, passion, voice, emotions, release, safety, escape, identity, compassion, and relatability to ALL. How can we not ensure that every one of our students has access to this? See figure 3.1 for a list of the benefits.

HIGH-QUALITY, STANDARDS-BASED MUSIC EDUCATION

We need to consider what qualifies as **high-quality music education**. Moreover, who should benefit from a high-quality music education? I am sure you can already guess the answer—ALL students should have access to it. A high-quality music program will be current, relevant, meaningful,

Musical Skills	Lifelong Benefits
Analysis, Conducting & Evaluating	Critical Thinking Making Choices Student Choice or Ideas Student Input
Ensemble Experience	Build Self-Esteem Peer Relationships Social Emotional Learning Social Skills Teamwork Turn-Taking
Playing Instruments	Connections to Occupational and Physical Therapy Skills Gross Motor Skills Cross Hemispheric Development
Reading & Notating Music	Connections to English Language Arts skills (e.g., reading, writing, analyzing, form) Connections to Math skills (e.g., counting, subdividing)
Singing	Communication Receptive and Expressive Language Speech Development

Figure 3.1. This chart describes some of the musical roles incorporated in our programs and the lifelong benefits associated with each. *Source: author created.*

diverse, representative, authentic, age and developmentally appropriate, engaging, and allow opportunities for ALL students to connect and identify with.

As mentioned in the previous chapter, I use the National Core Arts Standards to create a high-quality, **standards-based music education** experience for ALL. In addition, I ensure that every student is exposed to a curriculum that meets the needs listed above and directly correlates to the National Core Arts Standards. Music teachers should ensure that their lessons are connected to the standards assigned by their school district and administration. For example, in New York City, we also have the NYC Blueprint for the Arts in Music. My music classroom and curriculum directly connect to the National and NYC Standards to ensure a high-quality and rigorous music education experience for ALL.

In addition, note the connection between music education and the Every Student Succeeds Act (ESSA). In the language of this federal law, music is expected to be part of every student's academic experience to create a well-rounded education. The National Association for Music Education has provided resources on the implications of ESSA and recommendations on how schools and programs should incorporate it.[3]

To summarize, every student should have access to high-quality, standards-based music education, as per ESSA. This includes students in general and special education. Just because students may be placed in a more restrictive environment or require modifications to their educational experience does not mean that the music education program should not allow them to reach their full potential. Music teachers can easily create an experience shaped around ALL students' strengths and allow them to enjoy the endless benefits of music.

WHO IS THE TEAM?

Now that we have established the incorporation of an accessible, high-quality, and standards-based music program—who are the **key players** responsible for creating one? This is done with others and requires an entire team to work together. The ultimate goal is to create a music education experience that reaches ALL students in their own unique way.

Of course, this involves music teachers. Music teachers are responsible for creating, delivering, and engaging ALL students. In addition, music teachers need to work alongside **classroom teachers** and **special education teachers**. Especially when working with students with higher support needs, music teachers must collaborate with the team to ensure that the proper amount of support is used. Music teachers should also develop positive relationships with **administrators**. Administrators (including principals, assistant principals, directors of visual and performing arts, and directors of special education) should be allies to help the music program and ALL individual students.

Music teachers should get used to regularly collaborating with **related service providers**. Related service providers are specialty therapists who work with students on specific targeted goals listed in a student's IEP. The related services provided for each student are mandated, meaning that each student has a scheduled number of sessions that must be met each week. Although it is true that sometimes music teachers can find students being pulled out of class for related services, ALL students are entitled to partake in music class. Music and related service providers can work together efficiently to best support each student and showcase how music can meet each area's specific needs. It is suggested that music teachers speak with related service providers if students miss music classes or even suggest pushing in and collaborating. Some examples of related service providers include

- speech language pathologists (SLPs)
- occupational therapists
- physical therapists
- counselors or social workers
- hearing therapists
- vision therapists
- music therapists
- art therapists

Music teachers should also be ready to collaborate with **paraprofessionals** and **teaching assistants**. Teaching assistants are usually found in elementary or younger grades. They are there to help assist and can be great team players to help lead small groups or ensembles. Paraprofessionals are assigned to assist a student who has a disability. In most cases, a paraprofessional will provide 1:1 support for an individual student, as designated on an IEP. In a special education or self-contained classroom, there may also be a paraprofessional who assists with ALL students. Some classes may have several paraprofessionals to assist students. Examples of paraprofessional student support include

- health
- crisis/behavioral
- toileting
- language
- transition

Paraprofessionals are essential team members and can provide input and suggestions, as they are typically with the students ALL day. In a 2023 article for the *Journal of General Music Education*, music education researcher Rachel Grimsby notes that "often, collaboration allows individuals to feel valued as they share their knowledge and expertise to produce new knowledge, develop materials, or create plans of action that may benefit those they teach."[4] It is suggested that music teachers develop a positive rapport with paraprofessionals and build a solid partnership to help support ALL students. It is also advised to ask questions or solicit ideas from the paraprofessionals regularly so they feel part of the classroom culture and team. Occasionally, paraprofessionals can lead small groups or ensembles within the music classroom. Paraprofessionals are human beings; we can make them feel part of the classroom community by allowing them to share about themselves, including the music they connect and identify with.

Lastly, music teachers should develop a positive rapport with **family and community members**. Family members can help share a wealth of knowledge about students, including interests, motivation, and cultural connections. Family members can also be welcome to share their own musical backgrounds with the class. Music teachers should also develop relationships with **outside organizations and resources**. Many nonprofit organizations can help infuse music education support into ALL programs. Check with your local or state NAfME chapters for a list of what is available in your area.

UNLEARNING

Let us go back to the vignette mentioned about Adrian at the beginning of this chapter. What about team members who may have a bias against Adrian? What about your own biases? Do these impact the outcome of an accessible classroom? The answer is yes.

As human beings, we are often shaped by how we were raised, how we were taught, our families and communities, our cultures, and our own experiences. These aspects can ultimately impact how we feel, teach, make decisions, and view our students. In addition, we may have been taught strategies in our preparation programs for engaging students, repertoire, musical examples, or different teaching methods. But do ALL of these create a fully inclusive environment and a sense of belonging for ALL?

One strategy that music educators can use is **unlearning**. It is not that we dismiss everything that has shaped us or the way we were taught, but we may need to unlearn some strategies or ideas that may not help create an accessible classroom for ALL.

In their book *Unlearning*, curriculum specialists Allison Posey and Katie Novak say "we cannot allow educators and systems to decide that our students are not capable and then prevent them from accessing the very experiences that will allow them change the trajectory of their lives."[5] It is vital that ALL key players, including music teachers, recognize the approaches that may be harmful or create barriers for our students. Although these teaching techniques may not be intentional, we need to acknowledge that many students do not have full access to participate for various reasons, and sometimes, it is the approach of the key players that causes **unintentional barriers**.

When it comes to unlearning, several aspects need to be considered. How do we view our students, and how do we view our students who have disabilities? What language do we use, and does it represent them as human beings? What are our biases, and how do they impact our classrooms? And what is a strength-based environment for ALL?

DISABILITY MODELS

One aspect that music teachers need to be aware of, and perhaps unlearn, is their view of individuals with disabilities. As mentioned in the previous chapter, the word "disability" is not a bad word. Nevertheless, the idea of having a disability has been misconstrued in the media and society. Music teachers should be aware of the various types of disability models.

The **medical model** is one example: individuals without disabilities feel that they want to *fix the person* with the disability. In a classroom, this can be harmful for some students who have disabilities. Remember, we teach human beings, and every student is vastly different. Rather than focus on curing or fixing their differences, we can celebrate their strengths and provide them with tools to achieve their best.

The **charity model** is a second example: the consensus is to pity or feel bad for the person with a disability. Like the medical model, this can be harmful to students. Instead of assuming the worst about our students, again, focus on their strengths and what they can do. Even more, create opportunities where their strengths can shine.

A third example is the **social model**. In this model, the world around them disables the individual rather than the disability itself. As an educator, I can preach that I have seen this firsthand—and I am sure I have unintentionally caused this as well. It is not that our students cannot do the task, grasp the concept, or perform the music; instead, it is how we present it or how we ask them to perform it. This involves a lot of reflection by the music educator. However, it is essential to be knowledgeable about when we are the ones causing the unintentional barriers.

We also need to consider the **neurodiversity affirming model**. This model connects right back to the idea that nothing is wrong either with the word "disability" or with having one. Instead, our differences and individual unique strengths can be incorporated and benefit the world. Instead of assuming that students with a disability cannot make music, use their strengths in the classroom, which may benefit everyone.

Other models exist; however, I find these four regularly in the music classroom. In the book *Demystifying Disability*, disability rights activist Emily Ladau says that "each of these models is helpful in explaining the way that our society perceives and understands disability; but ultimately, disability is a complex human experience that can't be placed squarely into any one category."[6]

For a music educator focused on unlearning how they approach and view individuals with disabilities, remember, our students are human beings first. We should not treat them differently or engage differently because they have a diagnosis; create an environment that allows them to engage how they do best. Even more, ask and listen to them. Their voices are the only ones who can tell us what they need and how they need it.

LANGUAGE FOR ALL

Another area that music teachers need to be aware of is the **language** used about students and their potential. Because we are talking about human beings, we must be aware that our language can be harmful, ableist, biased, and detrimental to their academic and social well-being. The language we use matters and can impact every aspect of our classrooms and ensembles, such as our opinions, judgments, ideas, and ultimately, our teaching.

In the 2020 article "Why You Need to Stop Using These Words and Phrases" in *Harvard Business Review*, associate editor Arni Ravishankar says "language is a tool we use to make sense of our feelings and environment. When we verbally describe the things, experiences, and people around us we are also assigning value to them and that value impacts how we interact with each other."[7] Again, the language that we use matters. Instead of assuming that our students *can't*, *won't*, are *unable to*, or *will not*, consider the barriers preventing them from achieving success and how we can remove those barriers for everyone.

Individuals with disabilities are impacted by two main types of language. **Person-first language (PFL)** recognizes that they are human beings first, and we should recognize them as a person before their disability is mentioned. When we use deficit-based language that does not recognize a student's possibilities, we take humanity away from them. Using Adrian as an example,

- He is a student with autism (rather than autistic student).
- He has higher support needs (rather than low functioning student).
- He is a nonspeaking student (rather than nonverbal student).

Similarly, some prefer to use **identify-first language (IFL)**. In some communities, they prefer to be recognized first by their disability, as some prefer to be recognized by their identified pronouns. For example, many in the autism or Deaf communities prefer to use IFL. Note that we cannot decide for those not part of that community. That is a personal choice that can only be made by that individual.

Regarding the use of PFL and IFL, current discussion is about which one should be used first because it connects back to models of disability, and members of the disability community share what is best. The common consensus is that nondisabled individuals should use PFL first unless a specific person asks to use IFL. It is OK to inquire how someone may want to be recognized—we want to create an environment where everyone feels welcome and a sense of belonging. In this text, I am using person-first language to embrace ALL readers.

Music teachers must also be aware that some terminology schools still use is outdated and can harm our students. Some examples include nonverbal (use nonspeaking instead) or low functioning (use higher support needs instead). Although it can seem confusing why language is updated, keep in mind that members of the disability community are sharing how some language creates barriers. Music teachers should regularly stay up to date with current trends to ensure that ALL students feel valued and welcome.

ABLEISM AND BIAS

Another area music teachers need to be aware of is **ableism**. Emily Ladau defines ableism as "attitudes, actions, and circumstances that devalue people because they are disabled or perceived as having a disability."[8] From another perspective, Ellie Middleton says that

> ableism is a form of discrimination or prejudice against disabled people, based on the incorrect belief that disabled people are inferior or less capable than non-disabled people. It involves the marginalization, stigmatization, and exclusion of disabled folks in many aspects of life, including education, employment, social interactions, and accessing support.[9]

Someone who showcases ableism is an **ableist**. Unfortunately, our world is highly ableist. Even more, our classrooms demonstrate ableism; we must be mindful of what, how, who, and where this resonates.

For example, when teachers assume that a student cannot learn an instrument, participate in a festival or concert, or perform a folk dance due to having a disability—this is ableism. When music teachers do not set up an environment that allows everyone ample room to move around and then expect a student who uses a wheelchair to either not participate or find a different way—this is ableism. When a music teacher assumes that students cannot play an instrument during a drum circle and just gives them a dancing scarf to wave around, this is ableism.

Music teachers need to be aware of their actions when engaging ALL students. If a student cannot complete a task, taking their hand and doing it for them is an example of ableism. Instead, the music teacher can ask students if they need assistance and how they can help. In this way, students have a voice to either say yes or no and share what they need to be successful. Another example is creating an ensemble within a school of students only in a special education classroom. Although the intention is to give the students opportunities, the teacher still separates them from their general education peers. The music teacher could simply create an ensemble of any students who want to make music together.

Other key players may use ableist language about students in some instances. Remember, we must be our students' allies and advocates for their success. When we take a holistic, student-centered approach focused on what every student *can* do, we begin to chip away at the ableist barriers and showcase our students' creative potential.

Music teachers must also be aware of how their own biases translate into the classroom. In their *Inclusive Language Guide*, The American Psychological Association (APA) defines **bias** as "an inclination or predisposition for or against something." Similarly, the APA defines **implicit bias** as "an attitude, of which one is not consciously aware, against a specific social group, also known as implicit prejudice or implicit attitude."[10] These are both found too often in the music classroom.

ALL human beings have biases and implicit biases. Music teachers need to be aware of their biases and ensure that they come from a place of empathy and are informed about the needs and backgrounds of ALL students. ALL students deserve a music classroom where they feel safe, valued, welcome, comfortable, able, and ready to make music.

STRENGTH-BASED MODEL

In contrast to unlearning non-inclusive approaches, we can also use a **strength-based model** for ALL. But what are the non-negotiables of creating a strength-based and accessible classroom for ALL? These are some of my beliefs as an educator, and I hope they resonate with you.

One strategy is the use of **positive niche construction**. Thomas Armstrong says

> in the neurodiversity model, there is no "normal" brain sitting in a vat somewhere at the Smithsonian or National Institutes of Health to which all brains must be compared. Instead, there are a wide diversity of brains populating this world. The neurodiversity-inspired educator will have a deep respect for each child's unique brain and seek to create the best differentiated learning environment within which it can strive.[11]

When we recognize that everyone has strengths and create ways for them to be used, this is the best way of creating a strength-based environment. Armstrong names seven areas of positive niche construction, including

1. strength awareness
2. positive role models
3. assistive technologies and universal design for learning
4. enhanced human resources
5. strength-based learning strategies
6. affirmative career aspirations
7. environmental modifications

Music teachers must also incorporate an environment that **develops independence** and enhances **student empowerment**. ALL students can achieve remarkable outcomes. However, the proper support and strategies are needed to get them there. When students feel empowered, their true potential shines. This will increase motivation and levels of engagement.

In addition, student **voice and choice** go together with independence and empowerment. Gone are the days when it was about the teacher being the sole leader, and students were forced to follow. In my classroom, I act as a facilitator; however, at the core, it is a culture of *us*. Students have complete say and choice in every aspect of what we do, learn, share, perform, and how we do it. We grow together as a community through this.

This necessitates **solid teamwork**. As a music educator, we cannot do this alone. Working with the key players to support ALL students is critical to creating a strength-based and accessible classroom for ALL. For example, in my classroom, developing partnerships with ALL paraprofessionals has been the key to developing a culture where everyone can succeed. Because the paraprofessionals are the ones I work directly with, rather than teachers—we are the ones who create this together. In addition, parents and families are part of the process as well. We could only do this with them.

Lastly is the **belief that ALL can**. It may sound silly, but this is probably the hardest. Due to my biases, opinions, and how I was shaped—even fifteen years into my teaching career, I am still unlearning many things that impact my classroom. At the core, I believe every student can, and I will help them find a way to get there.

Now that we have broken down where we stand and who the key players are, what are the strategies for making our music programs accessible? Hopefully, you are comfy with a good snack. Let us delve into that in the next chapter.

CLOSING COMMENTS

At the beginning of the chapter, we read a vignette about a new student, Adrian, who would join Ms. Greer's music class. As she prepared for his first day later during the week, she heard from various colleagues about Adrian, which may have caused a bias or preconceived notion about him. Adrian's first day of music class went differently than planned. Afterward, she felt frustrated and even considered that he should not partake in music class. We used this example to explore further some of the unintentional barriers and biases that impact what happens in our classrooms.

We used the rest of this chapter to connect to those in the school community who may have impacted our thoughts about Adrian. We also discussed why we teach what we do and what is considered high-quality music education. We then addressed the idea of unlearning and different aspects of our classrooms that we need to be aware of. We ended by discussing a strength-based model and some ideas of what this would look like.

Now that we have gotten past the *who* aspect of our classrooms (ALL students and the adults), we are now moving toward the *what*. This is where the real fun begins. Our next focus will be the strategies to make our classrooms accessible for ALL. And then, after that, what does it look like?

REFLECTION QUESTIONS

1. In your music classroom, who are the key players most essential to develop a strong rapport with? How would you do so?
2. How can you recognize your own biases? How do you even know that you may have biases you may be unaware of? How can these impact your teaching?

3. What other areas that may not be listed would you incorporate to create a strength-based model?
4. What areas do you find yourself, your team, or the school community having to unlearn? How would you approach these?

NOTES

1. Andrea Cooper, "Cluing in on the Mystery of Music Therapy with Oliver Sacks," *Brain and Life Magazine*, February 1, 2008, https://www.brainandlife.org/articles/unchained-by-melody.

2. Judith Jellison, *Including Everyone* (Oxford University Press, 2015), 104.

3. "Policy Priorities," National Association for Music Education, accessed August 26, 2024, https://nafme.org/advocacy/policy-priorities/.

4. Rachel Grimsby, "Alternative Avenues for Collaborating with Special Education Paraprofessionals," *Journal of General Music Education* 36, no. 2 (2022): 13–19, https://doi.org/10.1177/27527646221130314.

5. Allison Posey and Katie Novak, *Unlearning: Changing Your Beliefs and Your Classroom with UDL* (CAST, 2020), 86.

6. Emily Ladau, *Demystifying Disability: What to Know, What to Say, and How to Be an Ally* (Ten Speed Press, 2021), 41.

7. Rakshitha A. Ravishankar, "Why You Need to Stop Using These Words and Phrases," *Harvard Business Review*, March 30, 2022, https://hbr.org/2020/12/why-you-need-to-stop-using-these-words-and-phrases.

8. Ladau, *Demystifying Disability: What to Know, What to Say, and How to Be an Ally*, 70.

9. Ellie Middleton, *UNMASKED: The Ultimate Guide to ADHD, Autism and Neurodivergence* (Random House, 2023), 169.

10. "Inclusive Language Guide," American Psychological Association, accessed August 25, 2024, https://www.apa.org/about/apa/equity-diversity-inclusion/language-guidelines?_gl=1*nlurrq*_ga*MjA2NTE0NDAzNS4xNzEzMDQwODQw*_ga_SZXLGDJGNB*MTcxMzA0MDg0MC4xLjAuMTcxMzA0MDg0MS4wLjAuMA.

11. Thomas Armstrong, *Neurodiversity in the Classroom: Strength-Based Strategies to Help Students with Special Needs Succeed in School and Life* (ASCD, 2012), 12–13.

Chapter 4

What Are the Basic Ideas?

ESSENTIAL QUESTIONS

1. How can music teachers incorporate universal design for learning (UDL), multisensory learning, assistive technology, task analysis, and conceptual learning to make the content more accessible?
2. How can music teachers provide multiple ways for ALL students to engage in musical settings?

CORE VOCABULARY

Planning and goals, backward planning, learning objectives, accessible learning objective, adaptations, accommodations, modification, generalization, universal design for learning (UDL), multisensory learning, assistive technology, task analysis, conceptual learning

OPENING THOUGHTS: VIGNETTE

Mr. Zimmermann is preparing to teach a first-grade general music class. For today's lesson, he plans to teach his students to sing the first verse and refrain to the folk song "Day Is Done" by Peter, Paul and Mary. To make things easier, he typed the lyrics of the text so he could showcase them on his SMART Board. ALL students will have access to the lyrics. He realizes that the font is not his favorite; however, it looks good from an audience perspective. He also retyped the lyrics to the first verse a second time, and as the second time the refrain appears, it says the word *refrain* instead of posting the actual words, and students can go back to where the lyrics were previously mentioned.

Mr. Zimmermann's first-grade class comes, and he begins by giving context to the song. He then explains that during the verse, the students are expected to stand quietly as that is not the focus of the lesson today. During the refrain, students will be expected to sing together. He models the refrain by singing it twice, then puts the musical track on and has students perform it. Afterward, he is shocked when only a handful of students perform the refrain, and even then, not confidently. He posted the lyrics and modeled the song but was confused about what had happened.

Think about the following questions:

1. Why did only a handful of students perform the song? Why did they not perform it accurately or confidently?
2. Was this lesson accessible to everyone? What unintentional barriers did you observe?
3. Assuming that you were teaching this selection, how would you change the way the activity is delivered?

Unfortunately, the lesson was not accessible to ALL. Some reasons include

- the font is not accessible to young readers
- first-grade students are expected to go back to locate the refrain text
- reading the text may be a barrier for some
- not every student may want to or be able to stand
- the verse was only introduced through modeling by singing
- not every student will perform it back through singing
- not every student may want to sing
- students had nothing to do during the verse
- the lyrics refer to comforting a *son*. Since not every student is a son, this does not create a sense of belonging and inclusion

Although the lesson was well-intentioned, it included many unintentional barriers. So what can Mr. Zimmermann do? How can he transform this lesson and make it accessible to ALL? Well, that is why we are here.

ACCESSIBLE LEARNING OBJECTIVES

When it comes to making our classrooms accessible to ALL, it starts with **planning and goals**. Although we are focused on creating high-quality and standards-based music education, it is also about how we clearly articulate our goals to ensure that students reach them. Music teachers are taught in teacher preparation programs to use Bloom's Taxonomy and the Depth of Knowledge Wheel terminology to help create these goals.

Music teachers are also introduced to **backward planning**, thinking about the result first and then working backward to create a sequential plan for getting there. Throughout the process, music teachers are also directed to develop **learning objectives**. Sometimes, you hear the terminology "learning goals" or "learning targets." These are the goals that students should be able to demonstrate in our classrooms. These goals should be clearly defined, measurable, observable, teachable, reachable, and achievable for ALL.

One of the biggest challenges that music teachers face is that their learning objectives are not clearly defined or worded, or they simply have too many ideas. If music teachers cannot clearly define what they want, how can they expect students to demonstrate it? When creating learning objectives, it may help to create a grid describing the learning objective, what students need to know previously, and what information students need to achieve to get there. Figure 4.1 showcases an example of what this looks like.

In his book *Preparing Instruction Objectives*, Robert Mager, who is noted for preparing instructional objectives, has simplified how teachers can break down a learning objective and articulate it clearly.[1] When

Learning Objective(s) or Targeted Skills	What do the students already know (prior knowledge, baseline)?	What do your students need to learn to get to the objective?
Students will sing the song Day is Done as an ensemble.	*Decoding text, matching pitches, singing from memory, using their high and low voices, etc.*	*Recalling a melody, recalling the rhythm, recognizing the verse from the refrain*

Figure 4.1. This example grid can help teachers consider the learning objective, the baseline knowledge needed beforehand, and the knowledge or skills needed to achieve it. *Source: author created.*

teaching my college students, I have them consider and clearly define five areas in their learning objectives. Each learning objective should only be one sentence long and should include the following information clearly defined:

Who? (e.g., individually, in pairs, in small groups, as an ensemble, with adult assistance/prompting, etc.)

What? (what are they learning specifically—e.g., the difference between legato and staccato)

How? (how are they learning it—e.g., through listening to repertoire examples by Brahms)

How well? (how well will they show you—e.g., is it a percentage; is it a certain amount of accuracy?)

When? (when will they show this to you—e.g., by the end of the class period, the end of the week, unit, etc.)

Let us go back to the "Day Is Done" activity. Assuming that we were to continue teaching the lesson the way Mr. Zimmermann taught it, a clearly defined learning objective may be articulated this way:

As a whole class, students will be able to sing the song "Day Is Done" with the lyrics provided with 85 percent accuracy by the end of the class period.

But let us back up a second. We also mentioned that not every student engages in the same way, and the lesson Mr. Zimmermann created was not accessible to ALL. What gives? We need to revise the learning objective and make it into an **accessible learning objective**. The difference is that we provide multiple different ways for ALL to engage. Remember, for us, engaging connects to the National Core Arts Standards four artistic processes (create, perform, respond, and connect).

In her book *An Attitude and Approach for Teaching Music to Special Learners*, distinguished music educator Elise S. Sobol asks "how many ways could a concept be taught so that even individuals who were the most compromised could learn it?"[2] At the December 2023 New York

State School Music Association (NYSSMA®) Winter Conference, I had the privilege to co-present the Requisite Understandings for Success in ALL Music Settings: Special Education and Support Services workshop with Dr. Sobol. She began the session by presenting the song "How Many Ways?" from the *Bean Bag Activities & Coordination Skills* CD by Georgiana Liccione Stewart. We listened to the lyrics during the music, asking how many ways we could hold a beanbag. We could hold it with our hands, feet, shoulders, and so on. The focus was that there are many ways to simply hold a beanbag.

This connects directly to our classrooms and teaching. We need to recognize that everyone learns in their own unique way; therefore, everyone needs a way to engage with the content in a way that works for them. Instead of presenting the content in a one-size-fits-ALL style, we can easily create multiple ways for everyone to have access. ALL students benefit from this.

If we were to revise our learning objective and make it accessible, it could be written as

> Individually or in small groups, students will be able to either sing, use gestures or movements, and/or point to demonstrate lyrical understanding of the song "Day Is Done" with 85 percent accuracy by the end of the class period.

In this revised accessible learning objective, students now have multiple ways to show their understanding of the lyrics. They can sing them if they want to. They can use different gestures, movements, or even American Sign Language (ASL). They can point to them (the lyrics, icons, pictures, etc.). What also makes it accessible to ALL is student choice. By using the words *and/or* in the accessible learning objective, students have a say in how they want to show Mr. Zimmermann. Student choice and voice are essential to making the music classroom accessible and empowering students.

Because this may be new for many, let us delve into some of the concepts to make our lessons accessible to ALL. In this journey, we may unlearn many of the strategies that were taught to us.

ADAPTATIONS, ACCOMMODATIONS, AND MODIFICATIONS

When it comes to making changes within the music classroom, key concepts include adaptations, accommodations, and modifications. Nevertheless, it is necessary to clarify the difference between the three. Many music teachers are not formally trained to incorporate these into the musical setting. This can feel challenging for many, as they are necessary to ensure success for ALL.

Clear definitions are listed in the *Continuum of Special Education Services for School-Age Students with Disabilities* through the New York State Education Department. They list accommodations as "adjustments to the environment, instruction or materials (e.g., instructional materials in alternative format such as large print or braille; fewer items on each page; extra time to complete tasks) that allow a student with a disability to access the content or complete assigned tasks. Accommodations do not alter what is being taught." In addition, it says that modifications "may be used to describe a change in the curriculum or measurement of learning, for example, when a student with a disability is unable to comprehend all of the content an instructor is teaching (e.g., reduced number of eight assignments; alternate grading system)."[3]

These three strategies are often listed on a student's IEP or 504 Accommodation Plan. This means that they are legally mandated in ALL class settings. The language in an IEP or 504 Accommodation often lists specific examples of what should be incorporated for each student's needs and goals. It is suggested that the music teacher become familiar with what is listed in each document at the beginning of the school year.

Let us break down these three definitions a little more. **Adaptations** are any materials, resources, strategies, or supports that can be used to allow a student to succeed and thrive. When teachers develop adaptations for students, they are individualized. Because every student is different, an adaptation is created to meet students where they are.

Accommodations are teachers' specific adaptations that allow students to reach the same objective as their general education peers. A common way of describing an accommodation seen in some literature is *leveling the playing field*. When a teacher incorporates an accommodation, the end goal is the same as for everyone else; what students use to get there or how they get there may differ slightly. For example, a student may need larger print music to perform a song. In addition, during a festival adjudication, a student may require a longer time to process sight-reading before she performs. In both examples, at the end the students showcase the same goal as their peers.

A **modification** is when we adapt and change the actual objective. Here, students may demonstrate a different goal than their peers. Using the two previous examples, a modification may be that the student only performs a section of the song while still using the larger print. In addition, the student may only be sight-reading a particular section of the music or performing only specific types of note values.

As mentioned, students with an adaptation, accommodation, or modification listed in their documentation have a legal right to have these honored. Music teachers can work with the special education team to create adaptations that best support each student. It is important to note that these supports should be age and developmentally appropriate, scaffold back to ideas previously learned, and, when applicable, be consistent with what is being used in other classrooms to allow opportunities for **generalization**.

It is essential to highlight that music teachers should not wait until they receive documentation that they need to create adaptations, accommodations, and modifications for a specific student. Remember—many students may have a non-apparent disability and may not have a formal diagnosis. Many of the ideas listed in an IEP or 504 Accommodation will benefit every student. Music teachers should get into the habit of presenting ALL music content in an accessible way and including multiple access points. This is only good teaching and should happen regularly for ALL.

UNIVERSAL DESIGN FOR LEARNING (UDL)

Music teachers may be unfamiliar with **universal design for learning (UDL)**. UDL is based on universal design from the architecture movement when the focus was on making buildings accessible. When first introduced to universal design, you may hear it connected to the curb cut of a sidewalk. The reason for a dip from the sidewalk to the street is so that a person who uses a wheelchair has access to get from one to the other. Even more, consider who else benefits from the dip in the curb: a mailperson pushing the mail cart, a parent pushing a stroller, a musician walking with an upright bass, or someone using a skateboard. Everyone benefits!

UDL is the same in our classrooms. UDL is when we remove any barriers to the learning or physical environment for a student with a disability, but the strategy benefits ALL learners. UDL can allow our classrooms and ensembles to become more accessible to everyone. If teachers would incorporate UDL regularly into their teaching practice, the need to segregate our students based on their learning needs would disappear. Unfortunately, UDL has not been a focal point in teacher preparation programs. We hope that this will change in the accessible arts education field.

UDL goes much deeper than simply thinking about how our strategies for the students with the most needs benefit ALL. In her book *UDL Now!* Katie Novak defines UDL as the "expression of a belief that all students are capable of learning and that instruction, when crafted and implemented with this belief in mind, can help all students succeed in inclusive and equitable learning environments."[4] This is the overall goal—creating a strength-based environment where every student is set up for success and the belief that ALL can.

In the 2023 article "How Universal Design for Learning Helps Students Merge onto the 'Learning Expressway'" for San Francisco radio station KQED, artist and educator Nimah Gobir says UDL "can be likened to a learning expressway with multiple means of representation, engagement, and expression serving as on-ramps, traffic patterns and off-ramps."[5] The Center for Applied Special Technology[6] has created guidelines titled The Universal Design for Learning Guidelines Version 3.0, which can be found on its website. These guidelines include multiple means of engagement, representation, and action and expression.

When music teachers get into the habit of allowing ALL students to have multiple ways to engage, our classrooms become more accessible. Everyone then can connect, learn, and showcase their musical ability in a way that works for them. The unique ways the musical content can be presented can help every student, not just those legally mandated, connect more deeply. As Dr. Rhoda Bernard says in her 2023 article for *Orfeu* and regularly, "necessary for some, and helpful for all."[7]

MULTISENSORY LEARNING

What different ways can content be delivered, and what do they look like specifically? One way to think of this is through **multisensory learning**. We have established how we ALL learn and experience the world in our own way. Think about how you learn a skill best. Some of us learn by hearing someone explain it. Others may learn by watching someone do it or reading about it. Others may learn by practicing the skill themself. Consider how you learn a piece of music. We could watch a live performance or YouTube video, listen to a recording, or practice it on our instruments by tapping and writing notes into our music.

When we engage using multiple senses, we provide numerous access points that ALL students can use to make music. Multisensory learning comprises four aspects:

Auditory—Can they hear it?
Visual—Can they see it?
Kinesthetic—Can they do it, or can they move to it?
Tactile—Can they feel it, or can they touch it?

Music teachers should consider presenting ALL materials and resources in multiple ways when creating lessons and objectives. Even more, music teachers should allow ALL students to respond in multiple different ways. This connects directly back to UDL. When we create multiple

Auditory	Visual
Backing tracks	Audio Visualizer
Listening examples	Color-coded notation
Metronome usage	Modelling
Musical cues and transitions	Picture icons
Musical repertoire as a tool	Pictures of items or instruments
Speaking or singing directions	Scripts
	Text printed or emboldened
	Visual images
Kinesthetic	**Tactile**
ASL (American Sign Language)	Assistive Technology
Gestures to represent words or text	Items students can touch to learn skills (e.g., blocks to teach rhythm)
Manipulatives to teach concepts (e.g., dancing scarves, parachutes)	Sensory items
Movement (e.g., clapping rhythms, tracing melodic contour)	

Figure 4.2. This table showcases the multiple ways music can be presented multisensory.
Source: author created.

ways to have access, we provide more opportunities for successful outcomes. Figure 4.2 showcases examples of multisensory learning.

ASSISTIVE TECHNOLOGY

When music teachers consider incorporating technology, they may first think about digital keyboards, laptops, iPads, tablets, and so forth. Although these are excellent ways to make music, the idea of accessible technology goes a lot deeper. It can provide many more interactive and engaging ways for ALL students to make high-quality music.

Assistive technology is any type of technology, device, manipulative, or support that allows an individual with a disability to have access to something. It does not have to be electronic. Assistive technology can range from low-tech (visuals, picture boards, recordable buttons, adapted scissors, and pencil grips) to high-tech (iPads, communication devices, motion-detecting technology).

Some types of assistive technology will be included in a student's IEP or 504 accommodation plan; as mentioned, music teachers are legally responsible for incorporating these. For example, recordable buttons can be used where teachers prerecord certain words to a song, and students can press the button to recite the words. Instead of verbalizing the words to a song, technology can become a way for students to have access to show that they are audiating the lyrics.

In some instances, music teachers may need to adapt the classroom materials to make them more accessible for some. For example, a teacher may need to adapt a xylophone mallet, drumstick, or viola bow. Velcro straps, gloves, or padding are just a few adaptations to help make the musical materials accessible. There are also many adapted music instruments, or attachments, that already exist that can be purchased. If these specific instruments or materials are added to a student's IEP, then the school district is responsible for purchasing them to allow that student to succeed.

In addition, many music technology devices and programs can also be used in the music classroom. Devices such as EyeHarp, Orba, Soundbeam, Specdrums, and Makey Makey are different ways to give students access to making music, in addition to Western traditional ways. These new ways of making music are not suggested to replace conventional Western instruments and styles; however, they are recommended to be used in addition to give more opportunities to make music in a way that works for students.

Although several types of technology can be costly, some are free and available online. For example, Creatability through Experiments with Google[8] provides accessible and free ways for students to make music. In one of their experiments, students can use their bodies through movement and a webcam to make music. Music teachers should check out West Music[9] for adapted musical instruments and can also use the Accessible Music Education Special Research Interest Group[10] through NAfME as a resource.

TASK ANALYSIS

Task analysis is when teachers carefully consider ALL the steps involved in a task and the sequential order in which they should be provided for ALL students to demonstrate independently. A simpler way of defining task analysis is to *break it down*. This can be applied to musical skills, concepts, ideas, curriculum, repertoire, learning objectives, and so forth.

When I introduce task analysis to my college students or during a presentation, I present them with a picture of two cubes. One cube is perfectly whole. The other cube is broken down into smaller cubes that, when put together, eventually make a second whole cube. This is a clear example of describing task analysis—the goal is to get to the whole cube, and we put the smaller cubes together to get there.

Music teachers need to carefully consider how an end goal is broken down into smaller steps and gradually put together into something more significant. For many students, which step comes first and in which order will matter. Task analysis should be considered when music teachers are planning their routines, as students should be able to predict the order of a sequence of events. Nevertheless, there may be instances when teaching a lesson that a student or class needs help understanding what is being taught. Instead of repeating the idea over and over, break it down into smaller steps—and break it down using multiple access points (there is your UDL connection).

For example, imagine that you want your middle-school instrumental ensemble to enter the classroom independently, get and set up their instruments, and prepare for your warm-up. Now, think about the many steps involved in reaching the end goal. For many students, this is too much to do independently and needs to be broken down into smaller steps. For some, the first step could be to *go get your instrument*. For others, though, the first step may be to *enter the music room*.

As we have discussed, everyone's brain works in a different way. Amazing things can happen when we can give our students the tools to get to where we want them to go. Empowerment and ownership can occur when the tools are provided to promote independence.

Here is a second example of a task analysis in action that I do with my elementary students. Part of our routine is learning the dance we are working on for our upcoming show. Rather than just getting them to their dancing spots and drilling the dance in, here is a sequential task analysis of how this small 10- to 15-minute routine is broken down:

- Review the movements in the dance (e.g., clap, stomp, tap knees, wave arms).
- Connect the four movements to a simple song (I use a karaoke version of "Row, Row, Row Your Boat"—changed to "Clap, Clap, Clap Your Hands," etc.).
- Apply these four movements to a song they are familiar with for generalization (e.g., "Can't Stop the Feeling" by Justin Timberlake).
- Model the focused dance with the moves in multiple ways (play a video with the audio track and connected visuals of the dance while modeling it on the stage—students have the choice of how they want to review the dance).
- Ask a student volunteer to model the dance, using visuals to highlight how they get to the stage and exit.
- Have the entire class dance and then sit back down.

Something as simple as that can happen in every music class, and it becomes part of the predictable routine. It is broken down step-by-step to provide multiple access points to allow the students to dance independently. Although this example showcases how this was preplanned, instances may come when students need additional support during the routine. For example, students may need this broken down even more in the final step. Maybe they need a visual task analysis of the following

1. Line up.
2. Walk backstage with your class.
3. Stand on the colored tape.
4. Walk to your dancing spot.
5. Perform the dance.
6. Take a bow.
7. Wait for the audience to clap.
8. Walk to your seat.
9. Sit down.

Every student is different, and their needs will be different. Remember, it is not that our students cannot complete the task. Identify the barrier, find a way to remove it, and use that tool to help support ALL.

CONCEPTUAL LEARNING

We also need to consider **conceptual learning**. Conceptual learning is when we create connections to musical skills using ideas, symbols, systems, languages, concepts, pictures, representations, or gestures connected to the real world. Simply put, we are using universal ideas our students are familiar with to build a solid foundation to engage. Universal ideas should be elements our students see daily and can easily be used to make connections.

Elise S. Sobol talks about her use of the upside-down stoplight. This system was used in ALL aspects of her teaching and classroom, building a stronger foundation for her students to engage with. She says

> this strategy offered a reality-based, systematic approach that united special education learning environments, whether a special area class in music or art, an elementary, middle, or high school classroom, a class in adaptive physical education, or work in the school store. The consistent use of conceptual learning with the colors red, yellow, and green helped students build applications for successful living.[11]

When using conceptual learning in music classrooms, teachers should consider what their students are already familiar with and how to use that to develop instruction. Conceptual learning can be incorporated into ALL aspects of the music classroom, including music literacy, conducting, composition, playing instruments, language and communication, transitions within and outside the classroom, behavior management, and so forth.

An example of conceptual learning I use in my classroom is the icons Go (green) and Stop (red). I specifically use these icons because they are found in my students' day-to-day lives, are part of their communities, and can easily connect to almost every aspect of my classroom. I specifically and purposefully use the colors green and red in multiple ways and in different areas of my classroom. Some examples of how I include them are

Music literacy—green, note; red, rest

Conducting—go to play or sing, stop to wait or finish

Dancing—walk from the green dancing spot and stop at the red dancing spot

Language—use a script with green words of what can be asked, and a different script in red with how to respond

Social emotional learning (SEL)—green sign for feeling ready to learn, red sign for needing a break

These are just a few ideas of how I use go and stop in my classroom. In the next chapter, we will discuss specific musical areas and conceptual learning in detail while also connecting to ALL the other basic concepts.

CLOSING COMMENTS

At the start of this chapter, we read a vignette about Mr. Zimmermann's music lesson and how it was not accessible to ALL. We next discussed that proper planning and creating accessible learning objectives are essential to creating a good music lesson. We then went deeper to discuss the aspects of making a lesson accessible to ALL.

We introduced the idea of UDL, multisensory learning, assistive technology, task analysis, and conceptual learning. We also discussed the importance and legal aspects of adaptations, accommodations, and modifications. Our primary focus point is that the strategies that are used for our students who have the most needs will, in turn, benefit ALL students. Music teachers should create accessible lessons ALL the time, with multiple access points for ALL students to engage with. When this happens regularly, ALL students can have access, equity, opportunity, and success in an environment shaped by their needs, interests, and strengths.

Let us go back to our vignette and consider how we can revise this lesson. Instead of just having the lyrics provided, Mr. Zimmermann can provide a slide on his screen with the text, with keywords from each line bolded and highlighted. In addition, a visual clip art or icon can be paired with each line and keyword. He can also develop a gesture or use ASL to represent that word and help recall memory. When it is time for students to show what they have learned, they have multiple ways to perform. They can sing the song if they choose, point to the icons or words as someone else sings, use gestures while someone else sings, or use a recordable button with prerecorded keywords. The students have multiple ways to take in the information and respond. Every student now has a way to have access to the lesson.

When it comes time to perform, every student might perform the song differently than the person next to them—that is OK. Every student can engage in the way that is best for them and what works for them. Even more, during the verse where students had nothing to do previously, they can use dancing scarves to keep moving, which can also help teach the form of the song.

In our next chapter, we will look at multiple types of activities we teach in the music classroom and ensemble and how each can become more accessible to ALL.

REFLECTION QUESTIONS

1. Can you think of an activity or routine in your classroom, and how you would use task analysis to break it down? Afterward, are there aspects that can be broken down even more?
2. How would you use conceptual learning in your classroom? What universal system would you use, and how many ways can it be incorporated?

3. What additional types of assistive technology would you use? How would you use them to make music?
4. Why do you think accessible learning objectives and UDL are not taught more in teacher preparation programs?

NOTES

1. Robert F. Mager, *Preparing Instructional Objectives: A Critical Tool in the Development of Effective Instruction*, third edition (Center for Effective Performance, 1997).

2. Elise S. Sobol, *An Attitude and Approach for Teaching Music to Special Learners*, third edition (Rowman & Littlefield in Partnership with the National Association for Music Education, 2017), 40.

3. "Continuum of Special Education Services for School-Age Students with Disabilities," University of the State of New York, State Education Department, and Office of P–12 Education: Office of Special Education, last modified November 2013, https://www.nysed.gov/sites/default/files/programs/special-education/continuum-of-special-education-services-for-school-age-students-with-disabilities.pdf.

4. Katie Novak, *UDL Now!: A Teacher's Guide to Applying Universal Design for Learning*, third edition (CAST, 2022), 19.

5. Nimah Gobir, "How Universal Design for Learning Helps Students Merge onto the 'Learning Expressway,'" KQED, May 13, 2023, https://www.kqed.org/mindshift/61731/how-universal-design-for-learning-helps-students-merge-onto-the-learning-expressway.

6. "The UDL Guidelines," CAST, accessed August 25, 2024, https://udlguidelines.cast.org/.

7. Rhoda Bernard, "Necessary for Some, and Helpful for All: Preparing Music Educators to Reach Every Student," *Orfeu* 8, no. 2 (2023): 1–15, ORCID:https://orcid.org/0009-0000-9636-8042.

8. "Creatability," Experiments with Google, accessed August 25, 2024, https://experiments.withgoogle.com/collection/creatability.

9. "West Music," accessed August 26, 2024, https://www.westmusic.com/.

10. "Accessible Music Education SRIG," Exceptionalities SRIG, accessed August 25, 2024, https://sites.google.com/view/exceptionalities-srig.

11. Sobol, *An Attitude and Approach for Teaching Music to Special Learners*, 43.

Chapter 5

How Do We Make Accessible Music for ALL?

ESSENTIAL QUESTIONS

1. How can music teachers use universal design for learning (UDL), assistive technology, task analysis, multisensory learning, and conceptual learning to allow ALL students to find success?
2. How can music teachers provide multiple ways for ALL students to have access to engage in musical settings?

CORE VOCABULARY

Universal design for learning (UDL), assistive technology, task analysis, multisensory learning, conceptual learning, age and developmentally appropriate, generalize, iconic images, color-coding, visual supports, theory of mind, listening maps, social story

OPENING THOUGHTS: VIGNETTE

Ms. Barker is preparing to teach her fifth-grade general music class how to play songs using the pitches B, A, and G on the soprano recorder. Her class has been working on recorder for the past month, and they already have musical knowledge of how to read rhythms and pitches from previous music lessons. She has multiple students with an IEP or 504 Accommodation Plan and multiple English learners in this music class. She is focused on preparing this new song for an upcoming informance for

62   Chapter 5

Figure 5.1.   This is an example of the exercise Ms. Barker prepared for her fifth-grade general music class to perform on soprano recorders. *Source: author created.*

parents. She decides to video record this lesson for her personal reflection afterward.

Ms. Barker has her class get their recorders and sit on the rug in front of the musical notation that she has prepared on her board. She has created her own exercise using the three pitches (see figure 5.1) and only uses half notes and quarter notes. The musical notation only has the first three pitch letters written under the first two measures of the song. She follows her typical routine: the class turns and talks about what they see, practices the pitches on their instruments without making noise, claps and counts the rhythms, and then plays. When the students perform the song, she is focused on looking at the score and using her finger to point to each pitch for students to follow while she sings the note pitches out loud. Some students master the song immediately, while others need more time to work on it. She figures that the class will just need to repeat the lesson several more times to have the song prepared to perform.

When Ms. Barker has free time, she decides to watch the video recording. She is surprised by what she sees in the video. Some of the students perform the song accurately. Some students need help finding the correct instrument pitches or following the rhythm accurately. Some students do not hold the recorder correctly, which results in their performance being less accurate. A few students do not have their recorders up to play and only realize everyone is playing by the time the song is finished. One student is sitting in the back with his hands covering his ears.

Think about the following questions:

1. Is this lesson accessible to ALL? Why or why not?
2. Looking at the score, what potential barriers do you see? How would you address these if you were to teach this lesson?

3. What additional strategies could Ms. Barker use to promote student independence and empowerment?

Although Ms. Barker had many positive aspects of this lesson, she could have incorporated many elements to make this lesson more accessible. This lesson also contained many unintentional barriers that Ms. Barker may have noticed during the video. Potential barriers include

- the way the music literacy was presented
- the type of information presented
- possible sensory overload with the number of stimuli presented
- the lack of review of how to use the instrument
- the need to provide more support to ensure student independence

THE ACCESSIBLE MUSIC CLASSROOM

This chapter is organized very differently from the previous ones. We are moving away from the *who* and the *what* aspects and toward the *how*. Specifically, how do we make the music we teach accessible to ALL in our classrooms and ensembles?

I want to put this disclaimer out there: the examples and strategies we will look at are *some* examples of how this would look. Most examples I will showcase are ones used in my classroom with my students. Your students will be different. There is no one way to showcase an accessible music classroom. Nevertheless, the strategies mentioned in the previous chapter can work with ALL age-groups and ALL types of music classrooms and ensembles.

By regularly incorporating UDL, multisensory learning, assistive technology, task analysis, and conceptual learning into your teaching practice, you provide multiple ways for every student to access the lesson. When you adapt your materials, repertoire, instruments, and classrooms, ALL students will benefit. This is not just for students who receive special education services and programs. This is how you can create access, equity, opportunity, and success for everyone in your music classroom.

When creating accessible materials for your students, ensuring that they are **age and developmentally appropriate** is crucial. Although the core strategies are transferable to ALL ages, they will look different depending on your classroom and students. For instance, if you teach a high-school music classroom with students who may be academically on an early elementary level, this does not mean that you are teaching them early elementary music. It is about recognizing them as individuals on their way to adulthood. You can modify the musical skills you teach, but you are using age-appropriate musical repertoire and supports, respecting them as near adults.

It is also important to highlight that the supports we create represent our student population and the real world. For example, when creating visual supports, the visuals that we use should represent ALL people. This includes people who are BIPOC, with disabilities, part of the LGBTQ-IA2S+ community, and ALL ages. Our students must see and identify themselves in what we use to make our classrooms accessible.

The rest of this chapter will focus on several areas of the music classroom and how they can become accessible. We will focus on music literacy, singing, playing instruments, listening, musical theater, and composition.

ACCESSIBLE MUSIC LITERACY

Musical notation is one of the primary curricular goals of a music program. Music literacy skills are showcased in ALL types of music classrooms and ALL age-groups. Many meaningful connections are simultaneously being developed when teaching students to read and notate music. Music literacy connects to reading, decoding, writing, analyzing, recognizing patterns and form, counting, fractions, subdividing, and more.

Although teaching students to read and notate music is important, consider the many potential barriers that may arise. Musical notation contains different shapes, symbols, icons, fonts, languages, pictures, numbers, letters, and so forth. For students who already may be struggling to connect with written language, music literacy can form another layer of barriers. It is important to note that not ALL students need to be able to read music to become successful and independent musicians. Plenty of professional musicians make high-quality music and do not read music.

Nevertheless, we should still expose ALL students to music literacy. Here are several ways to make musical notation accessible to ALL.

- Present music literacy multisensory
  - visual—color-coding, iconic notation, different size note values;
  - auditory—backing tracks, counting or singing out loud, modeling;
  - kinesthetic—body percussion, movement, gestures;
  - tactile—manipulatives, tapping, touching.
- Incorporate various types of technology to provide access.
- Incorporate task analysis and break things down into smaller chunks.
- Provide multiple entry points so ALL students can find success.
- Use conceptual learning (e.g., go and stop, rainbow spectrum) to build connections to musical notation.
- Incorporate Braille music if applicable.

So, what does this look like in action? As mentioned in the previous chapter, I use Go and Stop icons as a foundation for conceptual learning. To introduce these two new words, we explore the difference between Go and Stop with younger students. We use Go paired with music to move, use body percussion, or play instruments. We use Stop to freeze or make a quiet sound. We do this with multiple repertoire examples so students can **generalize** this skill. This is very similar to the concept of the game Freeze Dance—except we are using Go and Stop here to build a foundation.

Next, Go represents the sound of something, whereas Stop represents a sound of silence. We may use the Go icon to clap our hands and Stop to show a silence count or beat. Or we could use Go to tap a hand drum or shake an egg shaker. Go and Stop are the primary ways that I begin by introducing literacy. Students may see a piece of music with three Go signs and one Stop and perform it however they choose. Gradually, we mix up the examples to allow opportunity for generalization. We can also begin switching the Go sign to **iconic images**. Iconic images are pictures or icons that communicate what we ask our students to do. If we want our students to clap their hands, they will see a picture of clapping. If we want them to shake the egg shaker, they will see a picture of an egg shaker.

Next, we transition to color-coded music notation. **Color-coding** is precisely what it sounds like—giving context to the colors we use. I

66   Chapter 5

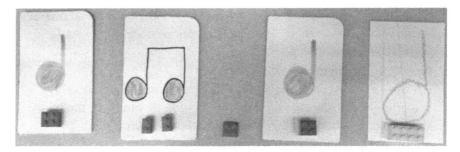

Figure 5.2. This is an example of color-coded rhythm flashcards using different-sized color-coded LEGO® pieces to add a tactile element. Source: author-created photograph.

introduce a green quarter note and a red quarter rest in this example. As you can see, green and red connect directly to Go and Stop. We are using conceptual learning to build an even stronger foundation. As we gradually add more rhythm values, you can color-code them however you want (I use blue eighth notes, purple sixteenth notes, orange half notes, and brown whole notes).

Musical notation can be presented in multiple ways. You can use the color-coded musical notation. Underneath it, you can use the Go and Stop images, iconic images, or both if necessary. Regarding different rhythm values, such as eighth notes, you can change the size of the Go or iconic images to make them smaller. You can also use colored LEGOS® connected to the color-coded notation to add another visual and tactile way to present literacy. You are presenting the information in multiple different ways (figure 5.2 presents an example using rhythm flashcards).

Here is an example of a task analysis of how this would work.

Musical Activity: "Billie Jean," performed by Michael Jackson

Age Range: General Music, Grades 6–8

Learning Objective: Using visual supports, students will be able to use instruments, body percussion, and/or rhythm syllables individually or in small groups to perform the accompaniment to "Billie Jean," combining quarter notes, eighth notes, half notes, sixteenth notes, and quarter rests with 85 percent accuracy by the end of the class period.

1. Introduce the music, artist, and background (I typically introduce the song title, artist, album, and year).

2. Listen to the music and see how many ways students can find the steady beat (I ask, "How many ways can you find the number four?").
3. Have a color-coded slide up with the numbers 1–4 and visuals of different movements that can be done with the body to show each beat (e.g., clap, stomp, wave, dab, floss).
4. Start the music and begin counting to four.
5. Model how we can tap each finger to count to four.
6. Model how we can tap the numbers on the screen or a printed copy to show the four beats.
7. Showcase the color-coded music notation (include icons or Go and Stop if necessary).
8. Provide multiple ways for students to demonstrate (body percussion, rhythm syllables, movement, instruments, or technology).

When it comes to melodic notation of pitches, a similar process can be incorporated. By using the colors of the rainbow spectrum, melodic pitches can be showcased in a conceptual way that again connects to something that is part of our students' lives. The rainbow is a part of nature, science, and our communities—and it can be used to make pitches more accessible. Even more so, many melodic instruments used in general music classrooms already follow the rainbow spectrum. Several assistive technology platforms also use the colors of the rainbow. Music teachers can also use color-coded stickers attached to instruments that connect to the rainbow spectrum.

In addition to using the colors of the rainbow, music teachers can showcase the melody's contour in multiple ways. For example, having students use their bodies to trace the melodic contour can lead to a deeper understanding of high and low sounds and transfer into a stronger performance when connected to literacy. Students can also have multiple ways to perform back pitches. Perhaps they can sing, perform on an instrument, use technology, use Curwen hand symbols, and so forth.

Some students may need additional musical cues, such as solfège syllables or pitch letter names connected to different notes. Remember, the goal is to promote independence as much as possible. If this is what students need to succeed, then it should be provided so that students can achieve it (figure 5.3 shows an example using colors from the rainbow spectrum).

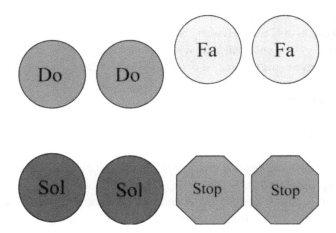

Figure 5.3. This is an example of color-coded circles using the pitches Do, Fa, and Sol, using the colors from the rainbow spectrum that can be performed in various ways. *Source: author created.*

ACCESSIBLE SINGING

Singing is integral to ALL music classrooms, including instrumental and performance ensembles. Singing can easily connect to ALL types of cultures and be used to connect to language, history, communication, identity, emotions, and socialization. Singing can be used as a precursor to performing on instruments and can allow students to internally develop musical skills before they transfer to other parts of the music classroom. Singing can also support students with language, communication, or social skills goals on their IEP, connecting to taking turns, diction, breath control, contrasting pitches, articulation, and so on.

As you may have considered already, many potential barriers arise in singing. Some students may be nonspeakers or emergent at vocalization. Some students may have sensory processing challenges, and partaking in an ensemble can be sensory overload. Some students may have difficulty decoding text or literacy, which can impact their musical performance. Some students may be anxious or uncomfortable singing in front of their peers or others.

A music teacher can consider many factors to make singing more accessible.

- Present singing multisensory
  - Visual—text provided, color-coded text, pictures or icons connected, ASL paired with text
  - Auditory—listening to recordings, backing tracks, self/peer modeling, hearing melody on an instrument
  - Kinesthetic—movement or gestures paired with phrases or text, ASL, using manipulatives to feel the form
  - Tactile—recordable talking buttons, iPad applications, objects to represent text or sections
- Assistive technology used to connect to keywords, text, or lyrics
- Incorporate technology such as noise-cancelling headphones to block out unnecessary sounds
- Manipulatives paired with singing and text
- Repertoire is chosen with which students are familiar, comfortable, and identify
- Repertoire is chosen that has repetition, clear form, and clear words/syllables
- Repertoire is age and developmentally appropriate
- Repertoire represents authentic diversity and exposes ALL students to new ideas

Let us look at an example I use with my students. I do this simple warm-up with my middle-school students before we sing. I have chosen these three warm-ups as they connect to many skills listed on the students' IEPs. See if you can spot potential barriers in these three steps.

1. How long is your voice? (Using any pitch, hold a sustained "ahh")
2. Can it go high and low? (Using the sound "ahh" or any other of your choosing, show how your voice can start low, glide to high, and then back low)
3. Can you sing the notes? (Sing a scale in solfège with a backing track)

I am sure your brain already is analyzing this. Many potential barriers exist (see the previous description; they ALL could apply here). Nevertheless, we can easily make this accessible to ALL.

1. How long is your voice?
   Have a green arrow visual, with tactile material such as Velcro that students can touch. Students can use their voices or hands to show long or feel the Velcro using their fingers or an object to make a sound. You can also connect technology such as the Spectrogram from Chrome Music Lab,[1] where students have a visual representation to show their voice.
2. Can it go high and low?
   Have a green arrow visual that shows the shape of going high and then low (an arch). Students can use their voices, their bodies to show the shape of high and low, or they can use technology. You can use Oscillators from Chrome Music Lab or Blob Opera from Google Experiments. Both examples allow students to use their fingers on a tablet or SMART Board to trace the shape. You could also use tablets where students can draw the sound of the contour into music.
3. Can you sing the notes?
   Students can sing, use Curwen hand signs, point to a visual solfège chart while the music happens, play it on a keyboard or small melodic instrument, use a tablet, or use a virtual piano to show that they recognize the pitches.

In ALL three examples, you now have multiple ways students can showcase something as simple as a vocal warm-up. But how do we do this with a song? Assume that we are teaching the refrain to the song "It's Okay" by Imagine Dragons. Here are multiple ways that the refrain can become accessible:

- Have the lyrics printed out and visible.
- If necessary, use icons for each word of the lyrics (some speech-language pathologists/SLP may have access to computer programs that may quickly turn text into icons).
- Color-code or highlight the keyword.
- Pair a visual with each line or section that connects with the keyword.
- Use a gesture, or ASL, to show the keyword while singing each part.
- For students who may be emergent speakers or singers, have them vocalize using vowels and consonants to the keyword only.

- Use recordable talking buttons or technology provided through SLPs, where students can press a button, and a prerecorded voice of the words will be presented.
- Students have the option to show how they want to perform the lyrics (sing, move, or use technology).

Music teachers should also consider what this may look like in a choral ensemble. Choral music and scores may contain additional potential barriers. Music teachers can exclude the other parts in a student's score, so they have less to process or focus on. They can also highlight specific parts, color-code, trace, or remove bar lines or unnecessary information that is not important or can be distracting. When teaching a particular part, music teachers should again present it in multiple different ways.

One example may be removing the music literacy altogether and teaching the part by rote. While this happens, music teachers can have students use their bodies to trace the melodic contour. In addition, music teachers can use markers to draw the shape of the melody before music literacy is connected. When the score is reintroduced, using a marker to highlight the melody can reinforce it. Other colors can be added to highlight specific details, such as rests, breath marks, dynamics, tempo changes, and so forth.

ACCESSIBLE MUSICAL INSTRUMENTS

Just like singing, ALL types of musical instruments can also be accessible. Musical instruments connect to culture, history, traditions, communication, ceremony, emotions, celebrations, and more. Musical instruments can also provide outlets for many students where words sometimes do not. When we consider what types of musical instruments are taught in most schools, we should recognize ALL types—including Western instruments, Eastern instruments when applicable, modern band ensembles, and musical technology.

When it comes to making music using instruments, many potential barriers arise. In most instances, students typically use their fingers, arms, or hands to make music. Students may also need to use their mouths, lips, breath, and embouchure. For some, students will need to cross their midline to be able to play a variety of pitches. Most instruments need to be held in a stationary position to make music.

Nevertheless, music teachers can adapt the actual instruments, the way they are played and manipulated, and how they are taught. Music teachers can consider many strategies to make instrumental music accessible:

- Adapt how to play, hold, or use an instrument (technique, supports, posture, embouchure, grasp, bow hold, fingering).
- Provide multiple ways that an instrument can be played (traditional posture, a student-chosen posture, something vastly different).
- Provide visual supports to promote student independence.
- Adapt music literacy.
- Provide assistive technology paired with instrument.
- Use age and developmentally appropriate supports.

Music teachers may need specialized equipment, attachments, or instruments for some students. For example, attachments such as a curved headjoint for a flute can be purchased to help some students who may need to use the instrument differently. Another example is adding pads to drums to dampen the sound for students who are hypersensitive to sound. Specialized instruments, such as a one-handed recorder, can be purchased. Remember, if a specialized item to ensure student success is added to their IEP, then it is mandated that the item be provided. West Music[2] offers many adapted instruments that can be used in ALL types of music classrooms.

Music teachers may also need to personally adapt instruments or change them. For example, a violin can be played at first, only using the two center strings (D and A) to provide less information and help students get used to developing their bow posture. A teacher can also move one of the strings into a different hole in the tailpiece to give more room between the strings. Specific manipulatives such as stickers or padding can be added to instruments for additional tactile support. For example, the neck of a violin can have padding purchased at a local pharmacy so students can feel where their thumb needs to go. These pads can be added onto the keys of woodwind or brass instruments or even drumsticks and mallets.

How an instrument is held, manipulated, or played must also be considered. Although music teachers should first consider adaptations or attachments to make the instrument more accessible, sometimes the instrument may need to be played in a nontraditional manner. If a student can make music successfully and independently while holding an instrument uniquely, then this should not matter. The goal is to make music. Many professional musicians play musical instruments in different ways. Even more, consider student voice and choice when first introducing an instrument. Ask them how they feel they would be most successful playing.

When it comes to using fingers to change pitches on instruments, this can also be a potential barrier. Some students may struggle to alternate their fingers independently. This could be an excellent opportunity to collaborate with occupational or physical therapists. The color-coded pitches mentioned earlier can be connected to the fingers used to perform music. A music teacher can use washable markers or color-coded circle stickers to place on fingers to help students match the color on their fingers to the color on their instrument. It is suggested that you always ask a student if this is OK.

Music teachers can also find other creative ways to get students to alternate their fingers. For example, in my string program, we found the song "Baby Shark" helpful for connecting to the fingers we use for different pitches. We then have multiple ways for students to demonstrate or describe each pitch (e.g., first finger, pitch E, or baby shark finger). If you were to do something like this, make sure that any song you incorporate would not cause trauma. Perhaps a student is missing a parent, and "Baby Shark" is not the best song, as the original lyrics may reinforce this. Changing the lyrics might work instead to teach the same skill but ensure that each student feels comfortable.

Visual supports are another great support that can benefit ALL. Visuals should be provided in ALL aspects of the music classroom; however, they can be extra support for making instrumental music. Visuals can be located wherever is best for the students, ensemble, and teacher. For example, a music teacher can visually represent instruments in playing and resting positions. The same can be said for visuals of what posture looks like, an instrument in its case, how a case or instrument is transitioned, and so forth.

Keep in mind that the visuals used should be age and developmentally appropriate. Visuals can be found online, in some method books, or taken

74   *Chapter 5*

within the actual classroom location. It may be best for some students to see a visual representation from their own perspective. Some students may struggle with **theory of mind**, which was coined by psychologists David Premack and Guy Woodruff in 1978. The idea of theory of mind is understanding a perspective that is not one's own. A music teacher can easily incorporate visuals showcasing what it would look like from a student's own eyes (figure 5.4 presents an example of how to hold a violin from a student's perspective).

Music teachers must also consider the language and vocabulary used in instrumental music. For example, orchestral directors use terminology such as *down bow* and *up bow* to represent when bows are moving side to side. For many, the words *down* and *up* may be taken literally. Instead, using terminology such as *wall bow* and *window bow* may help—or using other aspects of the classroom environment. Another example is when holding the bow of a stringed instrument, connecting to an animal such as an octopus to develop a more accurate bow hold rather than focusing on traditional terminology.

Lastly, using musical instruments typically involves many steps. These steps include setting up, getting into position, performing, and cleaning up. Many students may need more support. Music teachers can use basic strategies from task analysis, such as a checklist, to break this down into smaller steps. Once students master these skills, then the checklist can be faded. For some, the checklist may always need to be there, but if that is what allows a student to be successful, then it is necessary. A checklist

      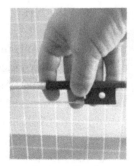

         Rest Position   Playing Position   Octopus Hand

Figure 5.4. **This visual represents what it would look like from a student's perspective to move from rest position to playing position and hold the bow correctly.** *Source: author created.*

How to Set Up Your Instrument	Finished
1) Pick up your instrument from the shelf	✓
2) Hold your instrument with two hands, and walk to your seat	✓
3) Turn the instrument case to the side, with the top facing up	✓
4) Open the latches on the side of the case	
5) Use two hands to gently pick your instrument up	
6) Take your instrument and sit in rest position	

Figure 5.5. This is a sample checklist for students to use to independently set up their orchestra instruments. It could be broken down even further or utilized with pictures or icons if necessary. *Source: author created.*

can use text, icons, or pictures of students demonstrating each step. See figure 5.5 for an example of a checklist used in an orchestra class.

ACCESSIBLE MUSICAL LISTENING

Teaching students to listen to music is also part of ALL musical classrooms. Music is consistently present in our lives in many different places, and we need to give our students the tools to listen and describe the music they enjoy. We also need to give our students the tools to use standards-based vocabulary to describe what they are hearing.

As with the other musical areas discussed previously, we can make musical listening accessible to ALL in many ways. Primarily, when we make music multisensory, everyone has a way to engage. While listening to a piece of music, students can move to describe what they are hearing or recognizing. Perhaps they use their bodies or materials, such as ribbon wands or dancing scarves. They could use these to trace the melodic contour or, as I call it, *paint the music.*

In addition, music teachers can incorporate visual and tactile manipulatives to help represent what students are listening to. **Listening maps** can be an excellent tool to give ALL students a visual representation of what is happening in the music. Listening maps can use symbols, icons, pictures, shapes, colors, and so on. Listening maps can also have elements where students touch objects to represent the types of sounds they hear.

For example, if they listen to a piece of soft music, they may touch a listening map with soft cotton or pom-pom balls. If students listen to something rough, they touch a piece of sandpaper to feel the rough sounds.

Music teachers can also incorporate technology to help represent musical sounds and find various and different ways to do so. For example, listening to a piece of music again through the Spectrogram on Chrome Music Lab might show the contrasting piano and forte sounds, legato and staccato sounds, and melodic contour. This can be beneficial to ALL students.

A musical example is "The Cuckoo in the Deep Woods" from *Carnival of the Animals* by Camille Saint-Saëns. This example uses only two instruments—the piano and the clarinet. Think about how many ways you can make this accessible for your students. Below is a task analysis of how this repertoire can become accessible to ALL.

Musical Activity: "The Cuckoo in the Deep Woods" by Camille Saint-Saëns

Age Range: General Music, Grades 2–4

Learning Objective: Using movement and/or listening maps, students will be able to individually describe the difference between the piano and the clarinet sounds in "The Cuckoo in the Deep Woods" with 85 percent accuracy by the end of the class period.

1. Explain the background of the music using a story, and pretend students are in a forest.
2. Play music and have students describe what they hear using visuals.
3. Have students locate the different instruments and point to the trees each time they hear the clarinet cuckoo sound.
4. Have students tiptoe around the room during the piano sounds while continuing to point when they hear the clarinet sounds.
5. Showcase a listening map that represents what happens in the music (I use one that has footsteps for the piano sounds and a picture of the bird for the clarinet).
6. Students can move, point to the map, touch the map, or have an individually printed map to show that they are following.
7. Students can create their own listening map by drawing or using items or movement to show that they can locate the different sounds.

Let us consider another musical example. In the "Raiders of the Lost Ark" theme from the 1981 soundtrack composed by John Williams, the focus would be to analyze and identify the overall form of the music. The actual form is rondo form (ABACA). This can be done easily by presenting the musical information in multiple ways and giving students various ways to respond.

Musical Activity: "Raiders of the Lost Ark" from *Raiders of the Lost Ark*

Age Range: Grades 4–6

Learning Objective: Using movement and visual supports, individually and/or in small groups, students will be able to identify and describe the rondo form sections in "Raiders of the Lost Ark" with 85 percent accuracy by the end of the class period.

1. Give background and context to the music.
2. Have students listen to the music with a visual listening map, representation, or technology showing the audio (e.g., Seeing Music from Creatability from Experiments with Google).[3]
3. Have students describe what they hear.
4. Use a parachute (or something similar) to have students move to the different sections in the music with visuals provided (I use up and down, fast waves, and spin in a circle).
5. Have students compare the different sections.
6. Have students use letters to connect the form using the visuals of the movements (the letters can be presented multiple ways; use color, shape, and letters). Figure 5.6 shows how the form letters can be represented in multiple ways.
7. Have students create their own rondo movement or composition to connect.

Accessible musical listening can also happen in an ensemble as well. Rather than just having students listen to an audio recording, music teachers can add elements to help make it more accessible and connect to the focus of contrasting audio clips. Using technology that showcases the audio visually can describe how different recordings may have different interpretations of a piece of music. These visual clips can also help students see specific rhythms that may be challenging to perform differently before introducing musical notation. Having students move in an

Figure 5.6. This is a visual example of how form letters can be presented in multiple ways: letters, shapes, and colors. *Source: author created.*

ensemble as they listen can help support a more accurate musical performance, as their muscle memory may be taking in musical information in multiple ways.

ACCESSIBLE MUSICAL THEATER

Although musical theater may not be found in every school or program, it offers many benefits for ALL students. I am highlighting this type of making music because I teach musical theater in my program and can speak from experience. Nevertheless, it is important to note that many of the ideas mentioned are easily transferable to an ensemble and into classroom music. Keep an open mind and consider what this might look like.

Although I am not trained in musical theater, I am an avid musical theater lover. Because I have lived and taught in New York City, this area connects to the culture of our professional arts community. I primarily teach in a center-based special education program, and there is something to engage everyone when creating a musical theater performance. My program typically puts on two shows yearly—one in December and one in June. My entire student population will participate in the musical theater production and performance.

When first introducing the show that will be performed, giving ALL students context and fundamental information is essential. Many students have anxiety, and this can help alleviate some fears of the unknown to make the process more comfortable. A **social story** can be created, which gives students basic information about what they need to know. Typically, a social story is used to help support behaviors (more discussed later). However, one can be created to introduce ALL information about the show. The social story should include visuals and be written in the first person so students can connect with it. Consider giving students the following information:

What is the name of the show?
Who wrote the show?
What day will we perform the show?
What time will we perform the show?
Where will we perform the show?
What will happen during the show?
Who will we perform the show for?
What is the show about?
How do you connect with the show?

It is important to mention where learning, rehearsals, and the performance will occur. If teaching in multiple locations within a campus, there will be a need to connect the skills from one location to the next for generalization. This can be included in the social story. Visuals can also be added in each area to help support student independence. For example, if students are expected to line up backstage, create a visual task analysis of how to get there (e.g., stand up, walk to the backstage door, stand on a line backstage).

When teaching the show content, ALL of these must be considered and how they would be accessible. Singing is one aspect of musical theater. Lyric sheets can be created with visuals to help support students. Other ideas mentioned previously during the accessible singing section can be transferred to musical theater.

Students may also need to learn dances in some performances. When teaching movement and dance, it is recommended that a multisensory aspect be used as well. Visuals can be paired for each move that correlates with the audio track. For example, if students move three steps to the left, they may see three footstep images. It is suggested that music teachers build a consistent visual vocabulary library, so visuals are the same for different dances. For example, a clap image will always be the same in different dances. This is also recommended in conjunction with music literacy.

It is also recommended that music teachers create structured visual supports of where students should stand when performing. One idea is to use colored dancing spots (typically used in physical education classrooms) and colored taped lines on the floor. Students then have a visual of standing on a spot located on a line. It is suggested that students practice this in the classroom before on a stage. Teachers can create an activity where students work together to create their own lines with the tape, choose their own dancing spots, place them on a line, and then learn the dance. Students can also have ownership of this, such as building the stage, setting up, and performing. See figure 5.7 for a script students can use to build a stage together.

Because movement and dance involve moving out of one space, using the four cardinal directions (north, south, east, west) can help connect to moving forward, back, and side to side. When creating a visual map of each dance, music teachers can use colored lines that connect with each movement (e.g., blue is north, red is south, yellow is east, and green is west). While students are following the moves using the map and watching the teacher, the color-coded lines can help communicate which direction they are moving.

It is also important to consider acting, reading a script, or using a microphone. Scripts can easily be adapted using visuals, colors, pictures, and so forth, to make them more accessible. Visuals such as Go and Stop can help students pace their speaking and know when to finish. Visuals can also help students use a microphone, such as communicating by holding it tall, speaking, not putting their lips on it, and passing it to another person when finished.

Teaching students how to respond and behave as audience members is also important. A visual guide can be showcased somewhere on the stage, near the seats, or on the walls, exploring different types of audience

Figure 5.7. This is a script for a student who will lead an activity asking their peers what color dancing spot they want as they work together to build a stage. Visuals can be paired with the script's text to make it more accessible. *Source: author created.*

etiquette. It is crucial to model this to students, alongside other school community members, as this is a life skill that can be applied to actual theaters, movie theaters, and so on.

Lastly, many ways are available to further build student independence. Hence, they have ownership and empowerment over the entire process of putting the show together and the actual performance. Color-coded show maps can be visible so students can follow along, see the order of the show's sequence, and know when to transition to the next station. This can also help support staff who may only be present during rehearsals. The same can be showcased with a map of where students will stand on the stage, using color-coded lines in conjunction with their stage spots (see figures 5.8 and 5.9 to see examples of these in action).

Music teachers can also develop student jobs throughout the process. For example, having a student director, stage manager, and scriptwriter can help increase motivation and engagement. Teachers can create job applications for each posting, where students apply and go through an interview process. This idea prepares them to apply for real jobs in the real world. Once chosen, students in each area can have different visual supports, such as checklists, to help them be as independent as possible (see figures 5.10 and 5.11 for examples of how to promote independence).

Scene & Song	Actors/Speakers	Singers	Dancers
Scene 1 & Song	Student A Student B Student C Student D	Singer A	Classes A & B
Scene 2 & Song	Student A Student B Student C	Singer B	Class C
Scene 3 & Song	Student A Student B	Singers C & D	Classes D & E
Scene 4 & Song	Student A Student B Student C Student D	Singer E	Class F

Figure 5.8. This example is a show map that could be posted where ALL students and staff can access it. The map communicates what scene is happening, followed by who the singer and dancers are. *Source: author created.*

82   Chapter 5

Blue Line (Stage 3)	1.	2.	3.	4.	5.	6.
Red Line (Stage 2)	1.	2.	3.	4.	5.	6.
Green Line (Stage 1)	1.	2.	3.	4.	5.	6.
Yellow Line (Microphone)	1.	2.	3.	4.	5.	6.
Orange Line (Below the Stage)	1.	2.	3.	4.	5.	6.

Backstage (Standby)	

Figure 5.9. This is an example of a color-coded stage spots map that can be posted backstage to help students see what color line they are standing on and where their dance spot would be. *Source: author created.*

Stage Manager Checklist	Finished
Set up 6 blue, red, and green dancing spots	✓
Set up 4 yellow dancing spots	✓
Set up 4 orange, and 4 purple dancing spots	✓
Bring out a music stand and the script	✓
Bring out the microphones, and the microphone basket	
Set up the props backstage	
Put all the costumes on the table backstage	

Figure 5.10. This is an example of a checklist for students to independently set up ALL the materials, props, and costumes for a performance. Connecting to go and stop, using green (left side) and red (right side) columns helps build a stronger foundation for the sequence of doing something and then finishing it. *Source: author created.*

ACCESSIBLE COMPOSITION

Allowing students to compose and create their own music is integral to ALL types of music classrooms and age groups. Composition will enable students to incorporate prior musical knowledge and encompass multiple aspects of creativity and student ownership. ALL students can and should

Assistant Director	Script Writers	Stage Managers
Job Requirements:	**Job Requirements:**	**Job Requirements:**
-Be in 8th grade	-Be in 6th, 7th, or 8th grade	-Be in 8th grade
-Meet with Mr. W once a week	-Meet with Mr. W twice a week	-Help set up the stage before rehearsals
-Help classes during rehearsal	-Be ready to stay focused, on task, and flexible	-Help clean up the stage after rehearsals
-Perform all scenes and dances with class	-Be ready to work with others	-Help move props and set pieces onto and off the stage
-Be ready to understudy if someone is absent		-Be ready to listen to directions
-Sing **one** song during the show		

Figure 5.11. This is an example of job postings for student leadership roles that they would fill out an application for and then interview for. *Source: author created.*

compose music. Musical composition can become accessible to ALL through many of the same strategies discussed throughout this chapter.

Composing music does not necessarily require students to use traditional musical notation. Visuals, manipulatives, items, icons, and so forth, can be valid forms of allowing students to create their own music. Perhaps instead of using notation, students may use colors, shapes, symbols of their choosing, letters, pictures, or something similar. Students may also use items such as colored tape, yarn, uncooked noodles, Popsicle sticks, construction paper, stickers, and toys.

The goal is for students to create music within the expected boundaries that the music teacher creates, directly correlating to the standards-based learning objectives. It should not matter if students are not using traditional Western musical notation if they can meet the same goals in ways that work for them.

> For example, assume we are doing a lesson on creating a composition exploring long and short sounds with an early elementary general music class. Below is a task analysis of how this could be accessible.
>
> Musical Activity: Long and Short Sounds Composition
>
> Age Group: Kindergarten–Grade 2
>
> Learning Objective: Using visual supports, individually and/or in pairs, students will be able to compose and perform a composition consisting of long and short sounds with 85 percent accuracy by the end of the class period.
>
> 1. Introduce/review types of long and short sounds.
> 2. Create a sound bank of long and short sounds (use vocal sounds, instruments, and items within the classroom).

84   Chapter 5

3. Have students take one whole piece of construction paper as their musical score.
4. Have students cut long and small strips of additional construction paper that can be glued or taped to their score.
5. Have students choose long and short sounds from the sound bank and apply them to their score.
6. Have students perform, share, assess, and more.

Similarly, perhaps students compose their own melodies in rondo form (ABACA). Before students are ready to transfer their melodies into actual musical notation, students can use colors from the rainbow to create melodies using the pitches required by the music teacher. For example, a visual sheet with circles reminding students to use the pitches La, Sol, and Mi can be provided for using colors to create their melodies. Each line can represent one section of the rondo form. Afterward, students can then use this as a reference when transferring it over into actual notation, alternative notation, or use this to perform (see figure 5.12 to see an accessible composition support.)

Older students may create their own lyrics or use poetry or text from elsewhere to create their own music. This can easily be broken down into notation by incorporating task analysis. Music teachers can begin by having students analyze the text of the song and figure out how many syllables

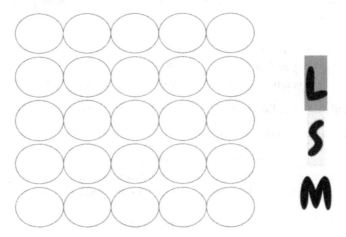

Figure 5.12. This is an example of a visual support where students can use colors to compose a piece of music in rondo form using the pitches La, Sol, and Mi. Each line represents one section of the rondo form. *Source: author created.*

are in each word. Students can then apply the types of rhythms they are familiar with and connect them to the number of syllables for each word. For example, a one-syllable word may be a quarter note. A two-syllable word can be two eighth or two quarter notes, and so on. Gradually, students can turn lyrics into notation. Music teachers can then have students add pitches and combine them into a song of a student's creation.

Lastly, consider the application of various types of musical technology. As described earlier, many free and accessible online platforms can be used for students to create their own music in many accessible ways. For example, using the Body Synth platform on Creatability through Experiments with Google can have students move their bodies to a computer screen to make sounds. Other online platforms, such as Incredibox,[4] allow students to create their own beatboxes online in a visual and accessible way that can be fun and engaging.

CLOSING COMMENTS

We began this chapter by reading a vignette about Ms. Barker's fifth-grade music class and her lesson on teaching her students to perform the pitches B, A, and G on the soprano recorder. We briefly discussed the lesson's background and approach and then analyzed where the unintentional barriers existed.

After this, we explored multiple areas within different types of music classrooms. We discussed many examples of how these areas can be broken down using the strategies mentioned in the previous chapter: UDL, multisensory learning, assistive technology, task analysis, and conceptual learning. It was emphasized that these strategies are adaptable and can be tailored to your own type of classroom, your students, your teaching philosophy and style, and the age level of your students. This flexibility empowers you to make your classrooms more accessible in ways that suit your unique teaching environment.

So, taking what we have discussed, what can Ms. Barker do to make her lesson more accessible? What strategies from musical literacy can she use? What strategy from musical instruments can she apply? Any other areas or suggestions? This self-reflection is a crucial step in your professional growth and development as a music educator, as it allows you to identify areas for improvement and implement new strategies.

Here are a few suggestions that could be applied:

- Take away the staff and measure numbers for less information to process.
- Use color-coded notation, and have the pitches listed in more places.
- Have students sing and move their bodies in the shape of the contour.
- Use color-coded stickers on the recorders that connect to the colors of the pitches.
- Incorporate technology where students can see a visual of their performance and see if the melodic contour connects to the shape of the melody.
- Have visual references accessible of how to hold a recorder.

REFLECTION QUESTIONS

1. What other areas exist within music classrooms, ensembles, or studios? What other ways can you use the accessible strategies, and how would they benefit ALL?
2. What one takeaway would you start with in your lessons to make them more accessible? How would you incorporate it?
3. Think of a lesson you taught previously or are preparing to teach—how would you alter this lesson using some of these strategies to make it more accessible to ALL?

NOTES

1. "Chrome Music Lab," Google, accessed August 25, 2024, https://musiclab.chromeexperiments.com/Experiments.
2. "West Music," accessed August 26, 2024, https://www.westmusic.com/.
3. "Creatability," Experiments with Google, accessed August 25, 2024, https://experiments.withgoogle.com/collection/creatability.
4. "Incredibox," accessed August 25, 2024, https://www.incredibox.com/.

Chapter 6

How Do We Enhance Lifelong Learning in the Process for ALL?

ESSENTIAL QUESTIONS

1. How can music educators facilitate lifelong learning for ALL through high-quality and standards-based music-making?
2. How can music educators empower ALL students through music?

CORE VOCABULARY

Lifelong learning, generalization, anchor standard #11, making connections, repertoire, cognition, input, retention, output, splinter skills, language, communication, receptive language, expressive language, nonspeakers, echolalia, immediate echolalia, delayed echolalia, whole language activities, scripts, augmentative and alternative communication (AAC), PEC symbols (picture exchange system), social skills, social emotional learning (SEL), mental health, emotional intelligence, emotional regulation, social stories, self-esteem, independence, empowerment, project-based learning (PBL), joint activity routines (JARS)

OPENING THOUGHTS: VIGNETTE

Mr. Safi is a first-year music teacher in a high-school setting, teaching general music and modern band. ALL his music classes and ensembles have students from general education, inclusion, and self-contained classes combined. Part of the school's focus is for students to converse independently in every class, including music. Mr. Safi has been trained to implement turn-and-talk routines in his teacher preparation program.

During a music lesson with an eleventh-grade class, Mr. Safi plans to introduce the genre of trap music, as he wants to incorporate music that the students listen to at home. As he begins to play a listening example, he can tell by the students' body language that they are more engaged than usual and some already know the song. He is excited to use this repertoire example to connect to the music curriculum that his administration has assigned.

After the students listen to the example, he plans to have them discuss their observations in small groups. His goal is for them to connect concepts such as rhythm, articulation, dynamics, form, and instrumentation and compare/contrast them to previous repertoire examples. Mr. Safi announces that students will have three minutes to turn to peers within their vicinity and document their observations to share afterward as a class discussion.

As he walks around during the three-minute block to observe student discussions, he notices that a handful of students are disengaged with their peers. He can tell that some students are not comfortable while others seem confused. He approaches one student and asks about their observations. The student responds that they do not know. A second student answers the question with a good observation; however, Mr. Safi needs to prompt them to share it with their group, who then agree with the observation.

Once the three minutes are finished, Mr. Safi asks for volunteers from each group to share their observations and then have the entire class compare their results. During this discussion, Mr. Safi notices that the same students taking charge in their groups are the same ones volunteering to speak in front of the class.

Think about the following:

1. What potential barriers did you observe in this lesson?
2. Did ALL students have access to participate in the discussion? Which students may have taken charge? Which students may not have been as engaged? Why?
3. What could Mr. Safi do to help make this activity more accessible to the students who need more support?
4. How would this be beneficial for every student in the class?

Although the lesson's intention seemed good, unintentional barriers were in the way when students were asked to respond. It is essential to highlight that Mr. Safi recognized the music that many of the students were interested in and used this as a tool to engage and teach the curriculum. Students will be more engaged when we use content they connect and identify with. We can still teach the same learning objectives with content representative of our student population.

The most significant barrier in this lesson was the implementation of the turn-and-talk. Having students discuss with their peers is a valid teaching approach and should be used. Nevertheless, Mr. Safi needed to implement additional strategies to help support ALL. Perhaps some students have anxiety and are uncomfortable talking around their peers or in front of others. Some students were processing the information and needed more time to formulate into words the ideas they wanted to share. Some students needed a cue to get them started so they could share their input. Even more, some students would have benefited from sharing their ideas in different ways rather than speaking their answers.

THE LEARNING PROCESS

As music educators, our primary focus is the musical curriculum assigned or developed. Our role is to ensure that every student we teach is learning, is safe, and has a pathway to success. Our teacher preparation programs focus on giving us the tools to develop high-quality music instruction. We are taught strategies for teaching musical concepts, conducting and leading rehearsals, developing concert programs, preparing students for adjudications and festivals, and scaffolding musical concepts across ALL grade bands.

But there is more to what we do than simply teaching music. Yes, music reaches ALL students in many ways, as discussed earlier in this book. But while we are making music with our students, we are reinforcing, connecting to, and teaching many other areas at the same time. Sometimes, we refer to this as the hidden, invisible, or secondary curriculum.

While we teach and make music, we also teach every student lifelong learning that they can apply outside our music classrooms. Although these areas can reinforce our students who have the most needs, ALL students benefit from developing lifelong learning in the process. In addition to what we do naturally, we can also prepare and give our students the tools to be independent citizens within our society.

Often, school administrators ask music teachers how they reinforce specific goals listed on a student's IEP. At first, this may seem overwhelming, as we may teach hundreds of students within one week. How can we ensure that we reach every student's goals while staying true to our content area? Do not be alarmed—we can easily meet a student's goals through making music. We can develop procedures and supports in our programs to become part of our natural musical routine. And every student would benefit from these, not just those with these mandated supports.

When we consider **lifelong learning** and learning in general, these involve multiple brain processes. In their 2015 article *Skill Development: How Brain Research Can Inform Music Teaching*, music educators Donald J. Walter and Jennifer S. Walter say that

> researchers have found that when someone learns a new motor skill, neurons in the brain create connections with other neurons at junctions called synapses. These synaptic connections link neurons together to create neural circuits that allow for complex actions. When people engage in many repetitions of an action, they strengthen their synaptic connections and create stable circuits for well-learned motor programs. In other words, "Neurons that fire together, wire together."[1]

ALL students learn in this way. We introduce a skill, we practice it through multiple repetitions, and we apply it. Think of this through the lens of music. Let us compare learning to sonata form. In sonata form, we start with an exposition section introducing a main theme. We later go through a development section, where the main theme modulates through multiple keys. We end with a recapitulation, where the main theme is restated but typically with a coda that adds closure.

Learning happens similarly. During the exposition stage, the new skill is introduced. During the development stage, students practice, repeat, and apply this skill in various ways. Finally, during the recapitulation stage, our students generalize the skill. **Generalization** refers to when our students can incorporate a skill into other situations or scenarios (see figure 6.1 for a visual representation of this process).

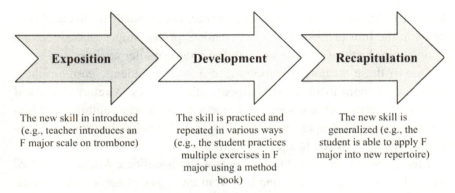

Figure 6.1. This visual representation connects musical sonata form to how one learns a skill and generalizes it to make connections. *Source: author created.*

For example, a student is introduced to an F major scale on a trombone. First, the teacher may introduce this scale through modeling, using literacy, or a method book. Next, the student may practice multiple exercises within their method book to get used to playing in this new key. Finally, the student can apply this to a piece of music while sightreading.

When we talk about learning a new skill, music teachers must keep several ideas in mind:

- The content should be taught in multiple ways.
- Students engage better when content is relevant and they can identify with it.
- Skills should be transferable to the real world.
- Skills should connect to goals listed on an IEP.
- The content should be age and developmentally appropriate.
- The content should be accessible and use UDL.
- Learning should showcase strength-based learning.

MAKING CONNECTIONS

As discussed earlier in this book, ALL music instruction should be of high quality. To ensure that it is so, our curriculum and teaching should directly connect to the standards listed by your district—primarily the National

Core Arts Standards. As mentioned earlier, engagement in this text connects to the four artistic processes: creating, performing, responding, and connecting. Each of these is broken down into smaller anchors.

One of these anchors is important to how our students learn and how music can benefit them in ALL aspects of their lives. **Anchor Standard #11** states "relate artistic ideas and works with societal, cultural and historical context to deepen understanding."[2] This anchor is critical to connecting what we teach to lifelong learning.

Elise S. Sobol says that "for students with disabilities, Anchor Standard #11 is key to bridging understanding from the music classroom to applications for independent living skills."[3] When connecting to this anchor, we are also teaching lifelong learning that our students can generalize and apply to the real world. When our music content is of high quality, culturally relevant, diverse, and student-centered, we can give our students the tools to help them become citizens in our society to the best of their ability.

Another way of considering this is by **making connections**. We use music as a vehicle or tool to build lifelong learning and connections for ALL students to use in the real world. We build this skill through modeling, practice, application, and generalization.

It is important to note that not ALL students have the independent ability to make connections yet. That is where we come in. Like our previous UDL examples, when we present ideas and concepts in multiple ways, we create multiple access points for ALL students to engage with and connect to. These types of connections will not happen automatically; they take time. Think like a musician—it takes practice.

Once a connection is made, we aim for students to use it in other examples and outside our music classrooms and ensembles. Some students may always need additional support or cues to get to that level of independence, which is OK. The goal is to develop lifelong learning for ALL through high-quality, standards-based music-making.

MUSICAL REPERTOIRE AS A TOOL

For music teachers, musical **repertoire** is the key to connecting our instruction to lifelong learning. Like other teachers use text, books, portfolios, and technology as their content, music teachers use repertoire. ALL the skills we can teach come from high-quality, culturally relevant, diverse, representative of student and community population, authentic, age and developmentally appropriate, and student-centered repertoire. The diverse repertoire chosen is not just for exposure or to say we hit a checkbox point, but a testament to our focus on inclusivity and respect for our students and their backgrounds.

Repertoire is more than just the songs or sheet music that we teach. It is the content that drives our instruction. Repertoire must be carefully chosen, and student choice and voice should be part of the process. Music teachers can easily teach the curricular goals using repertoire that may not be considered Western traditional. If we can meet our goals and engage our students in multiple ways while allowing them to feel a sense of belonging, then that is ALL that matters.

When selecting repertoire for instruction, music teachers usually consider the musical skills they want students to learn. Many of these skills will scaffold back to prior knowledge, allowing opportunities for generalization. Our learning objectives are derived from this.

Nevertheless, musical repertoire can go much deeper than this. When we consider lifelong learning and making connections, different types of repertoire and music-making can provide reinforcement in many areas. Such areas we will explore include cognition, language, communication, social skills, emotional regulation, social emotional learning (SEL), and developing independence.

As discussed previously, thirteen categories of disabilities are listed through the Individuals with Disabilities Education Act (IDEA). We also referenced the work of Alice Hammel and Ryan Hourigan in the six domains they list in their book. Making connections easily pairs with the six listed domains while still benefiting ALL students. In addition, when making connections, we reinforce the goals that may be listed on a student's IEP. Everyone benefits from making connections while making music at the same time.

COGNITION

Cognition is one area that music teachers must consider developing lifelong learning for ALL. The renowned Romanian Israeli cognitive psychologist Reuven Feuerstein helped the educational community understand how cognitive function and cognitive dysfunctions can be seen in our special education classrooms. Elise S. Sobol says *"cognitive function* pertains to thinking skills or mental processes. *Cognitive dysfunction* is a term used by special educators to explain the different functioning of three phases of our mental processes: the input phase, the elaboration phase, and the output phase."[4]

Hammel and Hourigan define cognition or cognitive function as "the generally accepted terms used to describe the ability of a student to receive, process, and commit information to memory." They also say

> for cognition to occur, a person must convert sensory energy into neural information. After this occurs, our perception utilizes sensory information to make further sense of the world (including our musical world). Finally, our cognition "involves the acquisition, storage, retrieval, and use of knowledge obtained by the sensory and perception systems."[5]

Many aspects of our students' lives can impact cognition. Some are born with them (e.g., traumatic brain injury), whereas others can be acquired at any time (e.g., through a car accident). Nevertheless, many activities and skills implemented through making music can positively impact cognition for ALL students.

When we consider cognition, there are mainly three areas. **Input** is the way our brain takes in and decodes information. **Retention** is the way that our brain retains information that is learned. **Output** is how we can generalize and perform information in various ways. Students can have challenges in one or even ALL these areas. Remember, ALL students are different, and their skills will be different. Always focus first on their strengths.

Some students may demonstrate what is called **splinter skills**. Certain types of skills that a student may demonstrate may not connect to the prior skills leading up to this. For example, a student may not be able to match pictures to a drawing but can independently complete a puzzle. In music class, maybe a student has a barrier of not being able to maintain a steady beat when performing together with their ensemble; however, when they are on a stage in front of an audience, they can perform accurately and with higher success than most of their peers.

It is important to remember that ALL students have strengths in different areas and will need support in others. Many strategies that can help develop cognition can benefit ALL students, not just students with specific needs. Some successful strategies that can facilitate cognition for ALL include:

- Information is broken down into smaller chunks (task analysis).
- Information is provided in multiple different ways (multisensory learning).
- Students have numerous ways to demonstrate a skill.
- Feedback is provided right away so students can generalize.
- Skills, behaviors, rules, and concepts are ALL modeled.
- Opportunities for cues to recall information are provided throughout teaching and lesson.
- Student voice and choice are incorporated as much as possible.
- Music is used as a tool to strengthen learning.
- Conceptual learning is used.
- UDL and assistive technology are incorporated.

For example, let us return to the vocal warm-up activity we talked about in the previous chapter. One aspect of the warm-up was asking students to sing a scale in solfège. As noted, a backing track of "Do-Re-Mi" from *The Sound of Music* was used for support. For some students, they may be able to sing the entire scale and use Curwen hand signs at the same time. For others, having them sing each solfège syllable is the barrier, as their output is the barrier. They know the sounds and they have retained them. However, the performance is where the barrier occurs that prevents success. Teachers can use "Do-Re-Mi" to facilitate a cue and have students fill in the blanks.

(S) _____
(T) a deer, a female deer
(S) _____
(T) a drop of golden sun
(S) _____
(T) a name, I call myself
(S) _____
(T) a long, long way to run

In this example, students know the pitches; perhaps they needed a cue to support the exact order or sequence. When music is used, it connects to a different part of their brain, and they can perform it independently. The music teacher can gradually fade this out as this skill becomes stronger. Nevertheless, the student may always need this support. If this is what they need to become successful, then it should not be an issue to use this as a tool.

Let us assume we were teaching a high-school modern band ensemble that had just chosen a new repertoire selection to work on. One student in the ensemble, though a talented bass guitarist, struggled to recall information learned from the previous rehearsal, and time was taken each class to reteach the content from the previous week. In this example, the music teacher could create a visual step-by-step checklist to help facilitate information retention and student independence. In addition, the music teacher can use colors in the sheet music for students to connect back to what was learned previously.

For example, green and red can be used for phrasing (the start of a new phrase would be green, and red would signify the end of a phrase). Shapes can be drawn into the music to give cues about what is happening in other parts throughout the song (e.g., a circle represents where the singer may have text, a square can represent a drum solo, and a triangle can represent an improvisation section). A chart can be posted on the board or handed out to each student, supporting the following information.

1. Review your rhythms, pitches, dynamics, and other musical elements.
2. Share with your ensemble your observations.
3. Take five minutes to practice your music on your own.
4. Perform with the ensemble.
5. Work together to add a new section to the music (use colors, shapes, and pictures in a way that works for you).
6. Practice again.

In this example, the supports were used throughout the performance aspect of the sheet music to help facilitate input and develop retention. Simultaneously, the checklist can help connect this lesson to the following lesson for a more substantial output. Every student could benefit from this tool.

LANGUAGE AND COMMUNICATION

Language is another aspect of lifelong learning that can be facilitated through making music. Consider how and why we use language and communicate in classrooms and throughout our day. What happens if we do not have access to language or communication?

ALL teachers and subject areas, including music, are teachers of language. Language is found in every aspect of what we do. Although there is much back and forth about whether music is a universal language, music can help become a language for some where words do not. As with other areas, music can be the vehicle to build tools to give ALL students access to the world around them. When our students have no access to language or a way to communicate, they have no way to interact with the surrounding world.

Language and communication go hand in hand. According to the American Speech-Language-Hearing Association (ASHA), **language** refers to "the words we use and how we use them to get what we want."[6] **Communication** is "the active process of exchanging information and ideas. Communication involves both understanding and expression."[7]

Language and communication are not only spoken words. We can facilitate language in many ways:

- visuals or pictures
- gestures or ASL
- facial expressions
- tone of voice or inflection
- technology
- pointing
- looking

Primarily, we use two types of language: **Receptive language** occurs when students can take in or process information; this is very similar to input in cognition. **Expressive language** occurs when students can use symbols of language to express their thoughts; this is similar to output. Just like cognition, some students may struggle with only one type of language, whereas other students may struggle with both.

Some students may be **nonspeakers**. Although "nonverbal" is still used in our classrooms and community, let us get out of the habit of using this out-of-date term. In a 2021 discussion with the Guild for Human Services, director of related services Corrina Riggs says

> I think those in the advocacy community (and many are self-advocates) feel that the term nonverbal is stigmatized because the general population equates nonverbal to not having or receptively understanding language. Many advocates want to change the narrative on that. Semantically speaking, the word nonverbal means without words, and there's pushback to say that nonspeaking individuals have words, but they cannot speak them.[8]

Everyone uses nonverbal communication at some point, and we need to consider what nonspeaking community members share with us about the importance of language. In a 2021 article for the nonprofit NeuroClastic,[9] which focuses on neurodivergent voices, several nonspeaking individuals shared why they prefer this term (see references). Just because some students may not communicate with spoken words does not imply that they do not have thoughts, ideas, opinions, interests, or things to share. They just need a different way to communicate. Other students may be emerging at vocalizing sounds and words. Music is a great way to connect and facilitate the work with speech language pathologists (SLPs).

Some students may have **echolalia**. This can be common for students who have autism. Echolalia is when language, dialogue, or conversations may be repeated within or outside the classroom. **Immediate echolalia** happens directly after someone speaks, and a student may repeat what was heard. For example, the music teacher may say to stand on the rug, and a student may respond, "Go stand on the rug." **Delayed echolalia** happens when a student repeats it afterward or out of context in the setting. For example, the same student may say, "Go stand on the rug" several hours later without any prompt. Some students may repeat dialogue they have heard on a TV show or a conversation they may have heard at home or elsewhere.

ALL students should have access to incorporate language and communication in the music classroom and ensemble. Music teachers should consider how many ways they can fuse language and communication into ALL aspects of instruction and making music to reinforce it. Many basic strategies such as UDL, multisensory learning, assistive technology, task analysis, and conceptual learning can be connected to build successful strategies to implement language.

In addition, **whole language activities** should be incorporated in ALL music classrooms and ensembles. Elise S. Sobol says that

> when teaching special learners, whole language activities through music include listening, speaking (singing), reading (notation), and writing (composing), creatively touching all four standards for literacy with the simplest of themes. Whole language's four-pronged approach encompasses four elements that are found in music.[10]

Whole language activities can be found in every aspect of what we do in music.

Listening: hear, touch, look, feel
Speaking: sing, talk, discuss, gesture, move, point, touch
Reading: notation, icons, colors, images, pictures, shapes, objects
Writing: compose, notes, objects, pictures, technology, improvisation

In addition, music teachers should implement many other strategies in their programs to infuse aspects of language for ALL. Music teachers can regularly collaborate with SLPs to find strategies best suited for the students within their programs. Remember to consider using methods that are age and developmentally appropriate. Recommendations include

- multiple ways to communicate
- gestures or ASL used
- augmentative and alternative communication (AAC)
- picture exchange symbols (PEC symbols)
- communication devices (GoTalk)
- iPad or other tablets
- scripts
- peer modeling opportunities
- microphones to represent taking turns
- conceptual learning strategies (e.g., go and stop)
- cue cards
- fill-in-the-blank strips

Having students independently engage with each other can be a barrier for some. Some students may need help creating a question, developing a response, engaging appropriately, or feeling comfortable enough to share. One suggested strategy is the incorporation of **scripts**. Scripts are structured to provide support, prompts, or cues of what to say, what to ask, or how to respond. Just like an actor uses a script to follow lines in a movie or play, a script in the classroom can provide an accessible means for ALL students to engage with each other. Scripts can be used in ALL aspects, routines, and locations within the music classroom (figure 6.2 shows an example of script prompts on a bulletin board wall).

Using the same vocal warm-up activity as earlier, music teachers can allow students to take ownership, take charge, and communicate with each other throughout this activity. Instead of the teacher being the activity facilitator, a student can be the peer teacher to lead the activity. A script can be developed to help the student lead, communicate, and engage with others.

(Student teacher) How long is your voice? My turn to show you. Ahhhh-hhhhh. Your turn.
(Individual or student group) Ahhhhhhhh.
(Student teacher) Great job because _____. Next time, try _____.

In another example, a student can lead an ensemble through an exercise in a method book with the same type of support. Students can have a schedule to create a task analysis on how to lead the ensemble. In addition,

Figure 6.2. This board on a classroom wall can support ALL students in knowing how to ask a question appropriately and independently and how to respond. The colors green and red utilize conceptual learning from Go and Stop. *Source: author-created photograph.*

scripts can be provided to have students lead the engaging questions and responses, allowing opportunities for critical thinking, as students will need to have reasons why they agree or disagree.

1. Analyze the music.
   (Student teacher) What do you see in the music?
   (Student) I see a quarter note. I see the pitch Bb.
   (Student teacher) I agree because _____. I disagree because _____.
2. Play the song.
3. Give feedback.
   (Student teacher) I liked it because _____. Next time, let us try to _____.
4. Ask for a soloist to model.
5. Give individual feedback.
6. Play again.

Scripts can be used to have students ask each other questions such as what instrument they want to use, who their partner will be in an activity, or what musical elements they recognize when listening to a piece of music. Scripts can be handed out individually when necessary or posted in accessible locations within the classroom for ALL students to access (see figure 6.3 for sample script questions and responses).

Using different types of prompts and supports can benefit ALL students. Prompts and supports include visuals or icons, PEC symbols, gestures or ASL, assistive technology, or musical cues. They can be used for ALL aspects of the music room, such as instruments, locations, basic needs and wants, and communication.

Some students may communicate using **augmentative and alternative communication (AAC)**. The American Speech-Language-Hearing Association (ASHA) refers to AAC as

> an area of clinical practice that supplements or compensates for impairments in speech-language production and/or comprehension, including spoken and written modes of communication. AAC falls under the broader umbrella of assistive technology, or the use of any equipment, tool, or strategy to improve functional daily living in individuals with disabilities or limitations.[11]

Let's give some **feedback**?

I can ask	I can say
Did you like it?	I liked it because _____
What was your favorite part?	I did not like it because _____
What can they try next time?	My favorite part was _____
	Yes No

Figure 6.3. These sample questions can be posted on slides or during a lesson to prompt students on how to have a discussion. The colors green (for I Can Ask on the left side) and red (for I Can Say on the right side) utilize conceptual learning from Go and Stop. *Source: author created.*

Students who use AAC will have goals written in their IEP by an SLP. Nevertheless, the strategies using AAC can benefit ALL students.

The use of visuals can be a support for everyone. Music teachers should have age and developmentally appropriate visuals around their classrooms. For example, different locations in the music room (the rug, keyboard area, instrument storage, computer areas, sensory area, etc.) should have visuals present to locate where the area is. In addition, ALL classroom materials should have a visual representation as well. Students can communicate when they want to use a guiro by speaking it, pointing to a picture, or pointing to the instrument itself.

Music teachers should also have a visual representation of essential words for students to communicate. Some examples include yes, no, bathroom, break, more, stop, finished. Some SLP teams may already have a visual board created that students can point to or use as support to communicate when they need something.

Some students will communicate using **PEC symbols** when assigned visuals that travel with them throughout the school building that they can either hand in or point to communicate their wants and needs. Other students may use technology such as GoTalk or tablets, which have purchased platforms for students to communicate. The SLP team will determine which method is best for each student.

Making music itself can also develop language and communication. Some basic musical strategies include

- Sing before speaking.
- Call and response songs teach taking turns.

- Singing, diction, vocal technique, and so forth, can help work with speaking tone and goals on a student's IEP.
- Technology and AAC can be incorporated into the music room.
- Visual supports can be used to represent text when needed.
- Words can be broken down into syllables or sounds while making music.
- Certain songs can have students input their ideas, words, and thoughts to develop expressive language.

For example, imagine we were working on the song "Green Eggs and Ham" from *Seussical the Musical*. The lyrics of the song contain connections with what happens within the storybook. Music teachers can have students communicate what they would not eat green eggs and ham with. Students can create new words (can even be rhyming words), draw picture representations, choose from a sample word/picture bank, use technology, or use a gesture to show it. In the end, students might show their example differently when they perform, but that is OK. Everyone can add their part in a way that works for them.

SOCIAL SKILLS

Like language and communication, music teachers need to consider **social skills** for ALL. Music teachers must reflect on whether ALL students have ways to engage and communicate with peers and whether their interactions are appropriate. We often assume that students have preset skills to navigate and engage with the world around them. However, this is not true for ALL. Some students imitate things that they see in the world. Others need a chance to be taught, practice, and apply these new skills.

Music teachers should also be aware that some students may enjoy engaging with their peers or with others, but some students may prefer the solitude of working alone. When doing activities in the classroom, perhaps students can choose to work with peers or alone. This way, they can complete the task in a way that is best for them or feels most comfortable.

Again, SLPs will be part of teaching social skills in the music environment. School counselors can also help teach students how to engage appropriately with each other. Many of the strategies listed under language and communication can be helpful for creating appropriate and positive interactions between students.

Music and repertoire selection can also be used to teach about friendship, working with others, understanding someone else's perspective, and teamwork. If a music teacher notices that social skills may be lacking in their classroom, selecting repertoire that targets these skills and developing secondary activities can help infuse positive interactions that students can generalize.

One example is the song "You've Got a Friend" by Carole King. The song's lyrics imply supporting a friend when they are down or troubled. The music teacher can teach the song and have students analyze and discuss the lyrics and their meaning. Afterward, students can work together to compose a new version of the lyrics to the refrain, talking about what they can do when they feel troubled and who they can reach out to. In addition, students can choose others within the classroom or outside and create a refrain about how they would help that person if in need. Music becomes the tool to develop these connections and create togetherness.

Another example is having precise and predictable routines, where a student volunteer can be empowered to lead the activity. When music teachers teach in the same way in each class, using the same vocabulary, students can appropriately imitate it back, which leads to positive interactions with their peers. This can happen in any age group and with any type of music.

For example, assume that you do a circle time activity in an early elementary classroom where students learn different ways to move their bodies with music. After going over each move, you can ask different students which move they want to perform with a song. Instead of the teacher leading this activity, a student can easily imitate this and ask others, "What do you want to do?" Something as simple as that creates the foundation for engaging appropriately with others.

SOCIAL EMOTIONAL LEARNING (SEL) AND EMOTIONAL REGULATION

Another area that music teachers need to be aware of is incorporating social emotional learning (SEL) and emotional regulation. Many students who enter our classrooms and ensembles may struggle to understand their emotions, what causes or triggers them, and how to respond. Even more, some students may need help understanding the feelings of others. Students who struggle to understand their emotions can also have challenges with behaviors that impact their performance in class.

SEL is a strategy that can help support ALL students in ALL aspects of their lives. The Collaborative for Academic, Social, and Emotional Learning (CASEL) provides resources that can be implemented in ALL types of classrooms (see resources). According to CASEL, "SEL is the process through which all young people and adults acquire and apply the knowledge, skills, and attitudes to develop healthy identities, manage emotions and achieve personal and collective goals, feel and show empathy for others, establish and maintain supportive relationships, and make responsible and caring decisions." In addition, they say that

> SEL advances educational equity and excellence through authentic school-family-community partnerships to establish learning environments and experiences that feature trusting and collaborative relationships, rigorous and meaningful curriculum and instruction, and ongoing evaluation. SEL can help address various forms of inequity and empower young people and adults to co-create thriving schools and contribute to safe, healthy, and just communities.[12]

CASEL lists five social core competencies that encompass SEL: self-awareness, self-management, social awareness, relationship skills, and responsible decision-making. Each state may have its own rules and regulations about incorporating SEL into schools. For example, in New York, ALL schools are required to implement SEL into the school curriculum. SEL can easily be connected and implemented into the music curriculum as well.

As noted by the thirteen disability categories in IDEA, some students may have a classified emotional disability. Many other students may have a non-apparent emotional disability. Some students may be struggling with challenges with **mental health**. The CDC mentions "mental health includes our emotional, psychological, and social well-being. It affects how we think, feel, and act. It also helps determine how we handle stress, relate to others, and make healthy choices. Mental health is important at every stage of life, from childhood and adolescence through adulthood."[13]

Recent current statistics showcase why SEL is necessary and relevant in school programs. According to a research article published by the CDC in 2022 regarding high-school statistics during the COVID-19 pandemic, 37.1 percent reported poor mental health, 44.2 percent reported sadness or hopelessness, 19.9 percent reported considered attempted suicide, and 9.0 percent reported attempted suicide.[14] Emotional challenges for many students have only increased due to the COVID-19 pandemic. According to an article published in *Chalkbeat New York* by journalist Amy Zimmer, 37 percent of New York City students were chronically absent for 10 percent of the 2022 school year.[15]

When it comes to incorporating strategies to support SEL for ALL students in the music classroom, music teachers can consider many supports:

- daily check-ins to see what students are feeling
- social cue supports
- social stories to teach appropriate behaviors or skills
- strategies to understand their own emotions or feelings
- strategies to cool down when they feel frustrated, angry, or upset
- scripts to help students learn how to communicate their feelings
- cooldown or sensory areas when needed
- individualized supports to use in specific scenarios
- opportunities for students to share what they need
- examples provided of others with emotional challenges and how they addressed them
- modeling targeted behaviors

One of the most critical elements of SEL is understanding one's own emotions and those of others. In his book *Permission to Feel*, founding director of the Yale Center for Emotional Intelligence Mark Brackett lists five necessary emotional skills to help promote **emotional intelligence**:[16]

1. recognizing the emotions of oneself and others;
2. understanding where these emotions come from;
3. using appropriate language to describe and label them;
4. being able to communicate with others our emotions; and
5. applying strategies appropriately (**emotional regulation**).

One strategy that his work has incorporated is the creation of the Mood Meter. Many schools and programs already use this system to teach students to recognize their emotions and use appropriate vocabulary to describe their feelings. Afterward, teachers can teach appropriate strategies to help students work through their emotions.

It is important to note that it is OK to feel specific emotions. Although we ALL want our students to be content and joyous, many obstacles and experiences in their lives can cause them to feel sadness, anger, fear, and more. We must recognize and validate what our students are feeling and allow them to know that it is OK to have these feelings. Only then can we work through these feelings rather than dismissing them.

For some students, it may help to create a visual, color-coded chart based on the Mood Meter using less vocabulary to build a foundation and gradually build from there. The Mood Meter is already color-coded (using the colors red, yellow, blue, and green). Basic emotional vocabulary paired with the colors can be connected to basic strategies for what a student can do when feeling this way (see figure 6.4 for an adapted color-coded version).

Another strategy that can be incorporated is visual prompts or scripts. Some students may need cues when responding to a situation or feeling a specific emotion. A visual chart can also be created and color-coded, giving students the cues of what they can say or ask during a particular emotion and basic strategies. These strategies are also connected to the

How am I feeling today?

Annoyed, worries or nervous?	Excited, proud or energized?
I can: Breathe Take a break Talk to an adult	I can: Ask to be a helper Help a friend Do some stretches
Tired, sad or bored?	Content, chill or relaxed?
I can: Talk to an adult Ask for something new Write down my feelings	I can: Do my best Help my teacher or friends Use kind words

Figure 6.4. This is a modified example of teaching students to recognize their emotions, connecting to the colors from the Mood Meter. Each color-coded box on the left contains different categories, and the right side provides strategies for each area. *Source: author created.*

Let's Talk!!!

When I feel angry, I can say	I need to take a break Can I take a walk? I need _____
When I need help, I can say	I do not understand Can you help me How do I do it?
When I want to talk to adults, I can say	I want to tell you about _____ I need _____ I am working for _____
When I want to talk to friends, I can say	How are you doing? That's cool because _____ I disagree because _____
When I want to play, I can say	My turn/your turn Good game! Let's play again

Figure 6.5. This is an example of visual support for students regarding what they can say or do when they feel a specific way and need a particular type of support. *Source: author created.*

language area mentioned earlier. In addition, visual supports can be showcased within the music classroom to help provide the tools to regulate a student's emotions—for example, incorporating a traffic light, with each color demonstrating different emotions and what they can do during that area (see figures 6.5 and 6.6 for examples).

Another aspect is the creation of **social stories**. Many students may need more specific skills and a strategy to help support them. Social stories are written in the first person; students can read them regularly to help replace a particular skill. Social stories should be age and developmentally appropriate and should be used regularly to build a foundation.

For example, assume that we have a student who is jealous when others get attention or specific materials, which would translate into a meltdown. A social story can be created explaining that it is OK to feel jealous. The story can then explain when a student has a meltdown due to jealousy, how it impacts the classroom, and how it affects their peers. The story can then discuss how and what the student can do when they feel jealous.

Making music and careful repertoire selection can also help facilitate positive SEL growth for ALL students. Basic strategies include

- Using music and repertoire focused on emotions
- Introducing musicians or composers with challenges
- Using music that students are interested in or motivated by

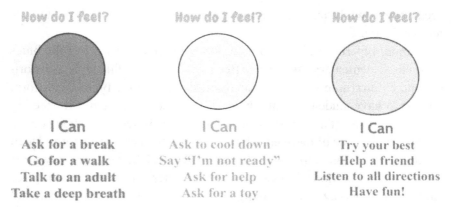

Figure 6.6. **This is a visual that can be posted in the music classroom. It connects to the colors on a traffic light. Each color represents a different feeling, with the strategies listed below.** *Source: author created.*

- Using as much student input in music-making opportunities as possible
- Using music to regulate emotions
- Composition and improvisation can be a perfect opportunity for students to create their own strategies through making music
- Being part of an ensemble can help with social cues and working with others

One area within the realm of SEL is the focus on **self-esteem**. Many of our students may have low self-esteem due to a variety of factors (age, disability, gender, identity, race, ethnicity, sexual orientation, socio-economic status, etc.). Many aspects and positive opportunities can be developed within the music classroom that can help support and increase a student's value of oneself. Opportunities to boost self-esteem are created when we provide opportunities to celebrate every student as a whole person using a strength-based approach.

One such repertoire example is the song "Roar" by Katy Perry. Imagine that a glee club version of this song was being prepared for an upcoming middle-school performance. While teaching the musical aspects of the song, the music teacher can go even further and discuss the importance and meaning behind the song's lyrics. The message of the song is about achieving goals and everyone having strength at something. A social story can be paired with the song, and students can have the opportunity to create their own lyrics or projects detailing what their strengths, interests, and goals are.

Another repertoire idea is to incorporate the musical style of the blues with early elementary students. After teaching about this style's historical and cultural importance, music teachers can use the blues lyrics form (AAB) to have students create their own emotional strategies for feeling frustrated, upset, or angry. Students can compose lyrics about their actions when they feel one of these emotions. Students then can brainstorm which strategies they can implement to help them feel better, cool down, or regulate their emotions. These composition lyrics can be used as tools for students to generalize when feeling these specific emotions (see figure 6.7 for an example of blues lyrics).

A final example may be transitional music within a class period. Students may be doing an activity involving movement, which will increase their energy levels. Music teachers can then plan a follow-up activity with calm or soothing music to help students regulate their energy and emotions and bring them back to a level ready to learn. Music can be fused throughout the lesson to increase and decrease levels gradually. Visuals or calm images can be paired during these cooldown activities to present information in multiple ways.

When I feel _____, I _____

When I feel _____, I _____

_____ makes me happy, and I feel great!

Figure 6.7. This is an example of how The Blues lyrics can allow students to share what they do when they are feeling upset, angry, or scared and create strategies to help support them. Visual icons can easily be used in addition to the text to make connections. *Source: author created.*

DEVELOPING INDEPENDENCE AND EMPOWERMENT

A final aspect of lifelong learning is developing **independence** for ALL. It is important to note that ALL students will have a different level of independence, which can mean something different for each student. Music teachers must be familiar with the goals be listed on a student's IEP. Nevertheless, the skills that are incorporated to promote independence can be beneficial for every student. Our goal is to create and promote a strength-based environment where ALL students can achieve their best.

Independence is accompanied by **empowerment**. ALL students should be able to take ownership of ALL aspects of the music classroom and ensemble. When students feel that their voices matter, their levels of engagement and motivation will only increase.

Student independence and empowerment can be found in ALL aspects of the classroom. This can include learning skills and content, setting up/ cleaning up, transitioning, following directions, and helping peers or others. Examples of strategies to help facilitate independence and empowerment include

- teaching content in multiple ways
- incorporating universal design for learning (UDL)
- incorporating assistive technology (AT)
- breaking things down into smaller steps (task analysis)
- incorporating visual supports for students (e.g., checklists)
- multiple repetitions of an activity, process, or routine
- modeling using adults and peers (positive role models)
- incorporating student choice to engage and motivate
- incorporating families as part of the process
- incorporating repertoire that allows independent skill-making opportunities
- having stations paired with visuals throughout your environment

One example is the use of visual supports and prompts. Visuals can guide independence and prompt students to complete a task. For example, assume that you want students to put taped lines on the floor to prepare to teach a folk dance. Visuals of each step include a) choose a partner, b) pick a roll of tape, c) one person holds the tape, d) the other person pulls the tape, and e) put the tape on the floor. In this example, students independently set up their stage rather than having a teacher do it.

In a musical theater production, students can have roles where they independently set up the stage. As discussed in the previous chapter, the color-coded checklist can give students the tools to know what needs to be set up and in which order, and they can check off each one as they finish.

Another example is having students choose a peer to go next during a classroom activity. For some students, this can be a barrier. The teacher can have a preset chart or visual with student names or pictures from which the student can choose. The chart can have two boxes—one box says pick a friend, and the second box is empty with a piece of Velcro. The student can select a Velcroed peer photo on the back of the chart and place it in the box on the front. In this example, again, students are independently making a choice but with the prompt that ensures success.

A further example is **project-based learning (PBL)**. Musical repertoire can be selected where students develop a team project or activity to learn additional skills. For example, assume that you were teaching the song "Going to the Zoo" by Tom Paxton. The folk song focuses on different animals found at the zoo. The class can work together to develop a project where they create their own zoo in the music classroom using art supplies. Different groups can independently create each animal exhibit. Once finished, the class would tour the zoo and connect it to the song. It could develop an even stronger connection if you take a field trip to a real zoo afterward.

While creating this project, the music teacher can collaborate with SLPs to develop **joint activity routines (JARS)**. JARS is a primary aspect of the Early Start Denver Model (ESDM, an evidence-based early intervention for children with autism). These are structured activities that help support social skills, language, communication, teamwork, and independence. Students would be able to work together to create their own exhibit; however, they may have the support of scripts and repetitive actions to help connect them to lifelong learning while completing their zoo project.

CLOSING COMMENTS

We started this chapter by reading the vignette about Mr. Safi's eleventh-grade music class. He introduced trap music to his students and noticed increased excitement and motivation. Nevertheless, when it came time for his students to discuss what they noticed in the music with their peers, he observed that the discussions were only led by a few students, where many others did not seem to be engaged.

We used this chapter to connect the idea of using high-quality, standards-based music instruction and the additional areas music can reinforce simultaneously. Our focus was that while our students were making music, we could teach lifelong skills that our students could generalize and apply to the real world. We discussed cognition, language, communication, social skills, SEL, emotional regulation, and developing independence.

The critical point to remember is that everything we do is age and developmentally appropriate and incorporates a strength-based model. Our goal is to empower each student in their own unique way while making music. When this happens, our students feel heard, relevant, connected, and welcome.

So, let us go back to Mr. Safi. What strategies could he apply to his lesson to facilitate language with students? Some ideas include

- Give students the choice whether they want to work in a group, with a partner, or by themselves.
- Post guiding questions somewhere visible.
- Have script responses to help facilitate discussion.
- Allow students multiple ways to create and share ideas (discuss, draw, move, show with technology, create a collage, etc.).
- Allow multiple ways for students to share their feedback with the class (e.g., create a word cloud using technology so students do not have to speak out loud).

REFLECTION QUESTIONS

1. What other areas of lifelong learning not discussed happen while making music? How would you support these skills in the music classroom or ensemble?

2. While these strategies may support students who lack specific skills, why is it important for ALL students to have access to them?
3. What other ways can you help students feel empowered in the music classroom? How do you think this will improve their self-esteem and value of themself?
4. Can you think of repertoire selections you may use that could connect to multiple types of lifelong learning skills? How would you create high-quality, standards-based instruction from it?

NOTES

1. Donald J. Walter and Jennifer S. Walter, "Skill Development: How Brain Research Can Inform Music Teaching," *Music Educators Journal* 101, no. 4 (2015): 49–55, https://doi.org/10.1177/0027432115574555

2. "What Are the National Arts Standards?," National Core Arts Standards.

3. Elise S. Sobol, *An Attitude and Approach for Teaching Music to Special Learners*, third edition (Rowman & Littlefield in Partnership with the National Association for Music Education, 2017), 69.

4. Sobol, *An Attitude and Approach for Teaching Music to Special Learners*, 8.

5. Alice M. Hammel and Ryan M. Hourigan, *Teaching Music to Students with Special Needs: A Label-Free Approach*, second edition (Oxford University Press, 2017), 14.

6. "What Is Speech? What Is Language?," American Speech-Language-Hearing Association, accessed August 25, 2024, https://www.asha.org/public/speech/development/speech-and-language/.

7. "Definition of Communication and Appropriate Targets," American Speech-Language-Hearing Association, accessed August 25, 2024, https://www.asha.org/njc/definition-of-communication-and-appropriate-targets/.

8. Corrina Riggs, "Ask the Expert: 'Nonspeaking' Vs. 'Nonverbal' and Why Language Matters," Guild for Human Services, November 29, 2021, https://www.guildhumanservices.org/blog/ask-expert-nonspeaking-vs-nonverbal-and-why-language-matters.

9. "On Using NonSpeaking, Minimally Speaking, or Unreliably Speaking over 'Non-Verbal': NonSpeakers Weigh In." Culture & Identity, Nonspeakers, NeuroClastic, effective August 21, 2021, https://neuroclastic.com/on-using-nonspeaking-minimally-speaking-or-unreliably-speaking-over-non-verbal-nonspeakers-weigh-in/.

10. Sobol, *An Attitude and Approach for Teaching Music to Special Learners*, 72.

11. "Augmentative and Alternative Communication (AAC)," American Speech-Language-Hearing Association, accessed August 25, 2024, https://www.asha.org/practice-portal/professional-issues/augmentative-and-alternative-communication/.

12. "Fundamentals of SEL," CASEL, accessed August 25, 2024, https://casel.org/fundamentals-of-sel/.

13. "About Mental Health," Mental Health, CDC, last modified April 16, 2024, https://www.cdc.gov/mentalhealth/learn/index.htm.

14. Sherry E. Jones, Kathleen A. Ethier, Marci Hertz, Sarah DeGue, Vi Donna Le, Jemekia Thornton, Connie Lim, Patricia J Dittus, and Sindhura Geda, "Mental Health, Suicidality, and Connectedness among High School Students during the COVID-19 Pandemic—Adolescent Behaviors and Experiences Survey, United States, January–June 2021," *MMWR Supplements* 71, no. 3 (2022): 16–21, https://doi.org/10.15585/mmwr.su7103a3.

15. Amy Zimmer, "'I'm Lucky If I Can Get Him Out of Bed': NYC Families Struggle with School Refusal," *Chalkbeat*, November 17, 2023, https://www.chalkbeat.org/newyork/2022/5/17/23099461/school-refusal-nyc-schools-students-anxiety-depression-chronic-absenteeism/.

16. Marc Brackett, *Permission to Feel: The Power of Emotional Intelligence to Achieve Well-Being and Success* (Celadon Books, 2019), 19.

Chapter 7

How Do We Create an Accessible, Strength-Based, Structured, and Predictable Learning Environment?

ESSENTIAL QUESTIONS

1. How can a music educator create an accessible learning environment for students with sensory, medical, or physical needs?
2. How can music educators understand the core function of behavior and implement evidence-based tools to replace targeted behaviors?

CORE VOCABULARY

sensory needs, hypersensitive, hyposensitive, sensory overload, restrictive and repetitive behaviors, hearing aids, cochlear implants, FM system, braille music, medical or physical needs, behavior, learned helplessness, attention seeking, planned ignoring, escape, behavioral intervention plan (BIP), extinguish, replace, positive behavioral intervention support (PBIS), classroom rules, consequences, procedures, routines, redirection, scatter plots, ABC charts, first/then charts, token economy system, individualized schedule, extinction burst, meltdowns

OPENING THOUGHTS: VIGNETTE

Ms. Hodge is teaching a listening activity to a fourth-grade general music class. One of the students in the class, Kimberly, has a diagnosis of autism and has an assigned paraprofessional. The paraprofessional and Ms.

Hodge have a cordial working relationship; however, the paraprofessional frequently gets frustrated with Kimberly.

Ms. Hodge is currently having students listen to the "Sabre Dance" from the *Khachaturian Gayane Suite* as students focus on musical dynamics. As the music plays, an interactive listening map that she has created is showcased on the SMART Board. In addition, she has students listen to the music in a way that works best for them and provides multiple options to engage. Some students follow the listening map; some listen with their eyes closed; some can move their bodies, whereas others have a board and dry-erase marker to draw what they hear.

During the lesson, Ms. Hodge notices that Kimberly is fidgeting her fingers in front of her face. As the music continues to play, Kimberly begins to rock back and forth, humming and disrupting the students around her. The paraprofessional physically moves Kimberly's spot on the rug, so she is sitting directly next to her. As the rocking continues, the paraprofessional tells her to stop and keep her body still, as it bothers the rest of the class. Kimberly's body language shows that she wants to return to her spot on the rug.

Once the music is finished, students will create an interactive representation of the music using shadow puppets highlighting the dynamics. As the class breaks into smaller groups, Kimberly starts to cry and bang her fists on the floor in frustration. The paraprofessional yells at Kimberly to stop and makes her sit out until she stops crying and is ready to join the rest of her classmates. Ms. Hodge frequently comes over to check on Kimberly. However, she notices that the crisis restarts each time she asks if she is ready to rejoin.

Think about the following:

1. What do you think was impacting Kimberly's behavior? What was the initial trigger?
2. Why did Kimberly's behavior continue to escalate throughout the music lesson?
3. What could Ms. Hodge or the paraprofessional have done to help support Kimberly?
4. How could this strategy help support ALL students?

In this instance, Kimberly is most likely hypersensitive to sound, which causes her sensory overload. Although it was great that Ms. Hodge presented the classroom materials in multiple ways, more was needed to ensure that the environment was accessible for ALL learners. The music to the "Sabre Dance" is loud and fast. For a student processing information at a speed different from others, this can cause sensory overload.

It also did not help that the paraprofessional, in this instance, moved Kimberly without asking and yelled at her to stop. As Kimberly was already having sensory overload, now she had to process this additional information of being moved, yelled at, and not being able to communicate what she was feeling or needed. This most likely escalated the crisis. Even more, while Ms. Hodge's attempt to check in on Kimberly was trying to be helpful, at this point this was adding more to the overload that Kimberly was feeling. It would have been more beneficial to give Kimberly the time and space to de-escalate on her own until she was ready to rejoin the class.

THE ACCESSIBLE MUSIC CLASSROOM ENVIRONMENT

Although most of this text has focused on classroom instruction, materials, resources, strategies, and activities, music teachers must also consider whether the classroom environment is accessible. This includes the exact location where learning, making music, rehearsals, and concerts are taking place. In many instances, what happens within the environment can pose unintentional barriers for many students.

Music teachers often have unique environmental situations. Some teachers may teach in multiple locations within one campus or even several campuses within a district. Some teachers may teach in their classrooms and the school auditorium. Other teachers may not have a classroom and need to push in to deliver instruction. No matter what type of situation the music teacher is in, it is critical to consider what the environment looks, sounds, and feels like.

Although many environmental factors may be outside a music teacher's control, there are other aspects they can consider when designing their space. Music teachers should view their location and ensure that ALL students have enough space to move around, and that the environment is distraction-free. If in a music classroom, this means making sure that the classroom instruments are stored away and not visible, and that papers and materials are organized and not lying around.

Considering what is showcased on classroom bulletin boards and walls is also recommended. Although inspirational posters can help boost energy and self-esteem for some, they can also be a distraction or become overwhelming for others. It is suggested that any wall space used within the classroom is specifically for making music or support, such as having a wall with cues of what to say or ask.

It is also recommended that centers or stations within the environment be created. Music teachers tend to have students transition in more ways than in a conventional classroom. This may include getting instruments, moving around, dancing, or standing on risers. If possible, create different labeled areas in the music room for various types of learning. It is also suggested that a sensory or cooldown area with materials be designed to help students self-regulate when they feel overwhelmed or just need a break.

STUDENTS WITH SENSORY NEEDS

Many students who enter our classrooms have **sensory needs**. When we think about sensory needs, we typically consider students with either hearing or seeing loss. Nevertheless, students may have many other sensory needs as well. Occupational therapists (OTs) can be great to collaborate with in schools regarding students' sensory needs. In addition, some students may have either hearing or vision therapists. These therapists will assign strategies and goals on a student's IEP, and as said before, music teachers are mandated to incorporate these.

The world around us, including our classrooms, is full of sensory information. This includes lights, sounds, smells, tastes, fabric, movement, locations, transitions, and temperature. Music classes contain many sensory stimuli that students need to process. Many classrooms also have sensory information from outside the room (e.g., the classroom is directly next to a schoolyard or distractions from a school hallway).

Typically, students may have two main types of sensory challenges. Some may be **hypersensitive**, meaning they are more sensitive to specific types of sensory stimuli and respond due to this. This can include lights, sounds, textures, temperature, smells, and more. Other students may be **hyposensitive**, requiring sensory input to help regulate their bodies to reach equilibrium. These students may require weighted objects, vests, sensory brushes, squeezes, or sensory hallways.

When students take in too much sensory information, they may have **sensory overload**. This may be when we see students rocking their bodies, fidgeting their fingers, jumping, or vocalizing loudly. When they reach sensory overload, students may demonstrate **restrictive and repetitive behaviors**. It is not that students are acting out or misbehaving; they are trying to expel sensory information to reach a level of equilibrium.

Consider it this way: a jar of jellybeans is half full, representing equilibrium. Once we add more jellybeans to the jar, and we want to get back to equilibrium, we need to get rid of some jellybeans to get there. On the flip side, let us imagine that we remove jellybeans from the original halfway line. To get back to equilibrium, we now need to add more. Sensory information and our bodies work similarly.

Sensory challenges can impact multiple aspects of a student, including behavior, language, and communication. ALL these areas are interconnected and can affect each other. A music teacher can make many considerations to ensure that the music classroom is sensory-friendly:

- incorporating amplifiers for hearing
- gestures or ASL
- directly facing students when communicating
- color-coding, enlarged font or print, and visual supports
- tactile manipulatives or elements to feel
- sensory input bins or areas in the classroom
- preferential seating
- instruments with muffled attachments
- incorporating high energy/low energy schedule
- setting up environment modifications where needed
- communication and collaboration with occupational, hearing, and vision therapists

Students who receive hearing services will require their own adaptations within the classroom. Some students may use **hearing aids** or **cochlear implants** to access the classroom contents. Some teachers may be required to wear an **FM system** to connect to this assistive technology. If a student uses this technology to have access and achieve success, then the music teacher is legally mandated to incorporate this into the classroom.

Students who receive vision services will also have their adaptations incorporated. Some may wear glasses or have various levels of vision loss. **Braille music** is a system of musical notation that can be helpful for students with vision loss. For a student to have access to braille music, a teacher trained in this type of literacy would need to teach it and use specialized technology to make accessible adaptations to sheet music. In addition, the student would need to become literate in braille music. Check with your local or state organizations to find where braille music and transcription services are located. For example, in New York, the Filomen M. D'Agostino Greenberg Music School offers musical transcriptions.

Sensory bins or stations within a classroom can be helpful. Music teachers can communicate with OTs to discuss what types of sensory materials are needed to help regulate students' learning. Examples include squishy items, items on strings, fidget items, slime, koosh balls, and sensory brushes. OTs may even provide support, such as sensory cushions on a chair or the floor under a student's feet. A location in the classroom can help students when they need to get an item or even wait there to cool down and regulate.

As discussed earlier, musical content can be presented in a multisensory way so that ALL students have multiple ways to engage. Music can be presented visually, kinesthetically, and through tactile elements. A student does not necessarily have to hear or see the music to engage with it successfully. Again, ALL students can benefit from having content presented in multiple ways and having multiple ways to respond.

Making music itself can also help regulate students' sensory stimuli. Suggestions include:

- using visual representatives (listening maps) for students to see or feel what is happening in a piece of music
- incorporating technology, such as Chrome Music Lab, for students to see what is happening in an excerpt
- using instruments, seating, placing, or objects for students to feel the vibration of music (e.g., balloons, rubber bands, Slinkys)

- using calm, soothing musical excerpts to lower the energy in a classroom, help with a transition, or diffuse a situation
- students using movement to represent sound, form, vocabulary, concepts, melody, and harmony
- incorporating songs and repertoire when a student feels overwhelmed or needs intake

STUDENTS WITH MEDICAL OR PHYSICAL NEEDS

Some students may have **medical or physical needs**. These may be diagnosed disabilities or non-apparent. Remember, students may be born with one, acquire it sometime during their lives, or even have it temporarily. The music teacher must ensure that the music classroom and performance location are accessible to ALL. It is also important to note that medical or physical needs have nothing to do with cognition.

Do not assume that a student cannot. Instead, ask what they need to be successful and find a way to provide it. This approach respects their autonomy and empowers them to take an active role in their learning. Focus on a student's strengths and create an environment shaped around these. Consider the essential elements of universal design and how this can create accessible entry points for ALL.

Students may have increased absences due to their medical needs. Students may also have restrictions within the music classroom that music teachers need to be aware of. For example, a student may need to use a school elevator rather than the stairs, or a student may need to be near a window in the classroom. Some students may require medication or feeding therapy. It is essential to be aware of student privacy laws and ensure that every student feels welcome and belongs in the music room. Music teachers must be aware of the limitations of participation listed on an IEP and ensure that these are honored.

Students with medical or physical needs may have paraprofessionals assigned to them to help support them. In addition, some students may have services through a physical therapist (PT) or other specialized therapists. Music teachers can implement accessible strategies to ensure that everyone can find success and collaborate with all therapists to ensure that goals are met in music. Accessible strategies include

- keeping the classroom organized so students can move independently;
- making sure the classroom environment is allergy (including food allergy) free;
- incorporating environmental modifications (e.g., no flashing lights);
- incorporating UDL and assistive technology (including adapted musical instruments);
- incorporating multisensory teaching;
- incorporating of historical examples of individuals with physical or medical needs;
- including activities that use crossing the midline and both hemispheres of the brain;
- activities that require a limited amount of movement;
- activities that consider the medical needs of a student;
- recognizing that student voice and choice are essential, and they can tell you what they need; and
- having a cooldown/break area in the classroom for students who need it.

As discussed earlier in this book, assistive musical technology and instruments can be used to ensure that every student has a way to make music. Music teachers can purchase attachments to instruments to help support, hold them up, or adapt the instrument. Many types of applications on tablets or websites are becoming more accessible to find new ways to give everyone access to making music. Music can be a fantastic opportunity for ALL students to shine and succeed. Music teachers should consider

- adaptive instruments so ALL students can make music;
- that students can learn about other musicians who have medical or physical needs and how they worked through their challenge;
- that students can be part of an ensemble, which will influence their self-esteem and allow them to work together with their peers;
- that students can use manipulatives (dancing scarves, ribbon wands, octoband, stretchy bands) to help with movement and cross-hemispheric development; and
- that singing should be incorporated as much as possible.

WHAT IS BEHAVIOR?

Another area in which many students may need support is **behavior**. Before we even delve into this area, what is behavior to you? How would you define it? How would you consider what qualifies expected behavior in your classroom or ensemble, and what would you think is either targeted, disruptive, or inappropriate?

In our teacher preparation programs, we may discuss basic classroom management strategies that can work. Still, we only sometimes talk about the function of behavior. *ALL behavior is communication.* That may not have been the answer you were thinking. However, research suggests that ALL behavior is a form of communication.

Sometimes, internal factors impact a student's behavior. These include sensory, medical, physical, and emotional aspects. In other words, things our students may feel internally impact their behavior. Other times, external factors can affect behavior. These are elements that are environmental or outside their body.

Because behavior is communication, what elements may students communicate to us through their actions? Examples include

- lack of accessible means to communicate;
- lack of understanding of the task asked;
- sensory needs;
- anxiety;
- needing more structure;
- learned helplessness;
- copying behavior;
- seeking attention;
- escaping from activity or work;
- needing tasks broken down more;
- needing individualized plans; and
- being shaped by previous experiences.

Although some of these elements may be familiar, others may involve new terminology. **Learned helplessness** occurs when a student gets used to someone else (adults or peers) doing everything for them. Sometimes, teachers and paraprofessionals unintentionally teach this. It is essential always to remember to promote student independence and empowerment, so students do not become dependent on adult support.

Some students may display **attention-seeking** behavior. They may demonstrate this behavior because they seek attention from adults or peers. It is important to note that negative attention (getting a reaction or consequence) is still attention, which may be what they seek. **Planned ignoring** can be a beneficial tool in some instances. For example, if a student is seeking attention by being disruptive during a music class, the music teacher can ignore the behavior until it stops or point to a visual redirection image without making eye contact with the student.

Other students may be seeking **escape** from an activity. They may find reasons or ways to avoid completing the task. Refrain from assuming that they do not enjoy music class—they may have gotten used to using this tool in other instances and are also incorporating it here. Remember always to incorporate student interests and strengths to help promote engagement and motivation.

When a music teacher considers why a student may be demonstrating a specific targeted behavior, three questions may arise:

> Why are they doing this?
> What function does this serve?
> What are they achieving in the end?

Music teachers need to stop categorizing behavior as *good* or *bad*. In their book *Music in Special Education*, distinguished music educators Mary S. Adamek and Alice-Ann Darrow say "behavior is a social construct, and there is no clear consensus on what constitutes good or bad behavior."[1] We need to look at the targeted behavior from a communication lens and determine how to answer the three questions listed above accurately. *Good* and *bad* are not definable; we cannot and should not categorize our students this way.

Regarding targeted behaviors, we need to stop assuming that our students *know better*. Again, behavior is communication, and a student may be demonstrating a targeted behavior as this is the only way they can communicate it currently. Our students are shaped by their previous experiences and pathways and communicate something to us through their choices and actions. Our job is to figure out what it is they need and help support them.

Music teachers must also get out of the habit of *my way or the highway*. This outdated mind-set needs to be revised to connect with students. It is often this philosophy, as well as the overall behaviors, that negatively impacts the culture of the classroom. We want our students to be engaged; to do this, they need to feel a sense of connection and empowerment. Find ways where their voice and choice can be part of the classroom culture. Otherwise, this will impact or increase the targeted behaviors within the classroom.

Music teachers must consider two contrasting words when discussing targeted behaviors that disrupt the learning environment—extinguish and replace. **Extinguish** implies that we are getting rid of the behavior. **Replace** means that we are creating a strategy to give students a new way to express themselves. Although extinguishing sounds like a better plan, it is important to highlight again that ALL behavior is communication. As ALL students have the right to communicate, we do not want to take that away from them. Therefore, replacement is the better option. We are teaching our students a more appropriate way to communicate their needs and help them get what they want or need.

Remember, some students have a **behavioral intervention plan (BIP)** as an amendment to their IEP. A BIP will be completed by a team within the school, and data typically will be collected to analyze whether the plan developed is working. If the plan is not working, then revision will happen. Students who have a BIP are also mandated to have it followed in the music classroom. Music teachers should communicate with the special education team to see how to implement it in their classroom.

Different schools and programs will have various types of behavioral methodologies in place. Typically, a team will help share the strategies that will be best connected to the method and what it looks like in each type of classroom. One type of system is **positive behavioral intervention support (PBIS)**. In his book *A Best Practice Guide to Assessment and Intervention for Autism Spectrum Disorder in Schools*, psychologist and cognitive behavioral therapist Lee A. Wilkinson calls PBIS an "approach that has evolved from traditional behavior management methods that are intended to decrease problem behaviors by designing effective environments and teaching students appropriate social and communication skills."[2]

The idea of PBIS is that ALL students can be considered in three categories. The first group comprises about 80 percent of the overall student population, in which basic classroom behavioral strategies will work. The second group includes about 15 percent for which specific plans or supports will need to be developed to achieve success. The final group, about 5 percent, consists of students who have a BIP. For our purposes, we will only focus on strategies for the first two groups.

BASIC CLASSROOM SUPPORTS

For about 80 percent of the student population, the primary classroom management strategies that the music teacher incorporates should work. This includes incorporating a structured classroom and routines, pacing, predictability, flow, contrasting and planned regulation of energy levels, in a strength-based and student-centered learning environment. It is also important to highlight that less targeted behaviors occur when students are engaged with content they relate to and have opportunities to feel empowered.

Music teachers need to consider incorporating clearly defined rules and consequences. **Classroom rules** are the listed expectations. Rules should be age and developmentally appropriate, posted in a location ALL students can access, and concise. The more language added to classroom rules, the more opportunities students have to find loopholes. It is recommended that visuals be paired with classroom rules. In this way, students can see a visual representation of what the expectation looks like. The teacher and ALL staff within the classroom should model ALL rules. Students need to trust the system, and if teachers do not follow it as well, why should students? For example, figure 7.1 shows the rules I use in my elementary classroom. They are short, definable, and easy to pair with a visual.

It is suggested that students help create the rules and expectations in the classroom. Although the word *respect* is often used, note that respect differs for everyone. Respect needs to be clearly defined, and even still, this can pose a challenge. An expectation may be OK in one culture,

Music Room Rules

Soft Voice

Listen to Directions

Sit Down

Gentle Hands

Walk

Figure 7.1. This visual represents classroom rules for an early elementary music classroom. The rules are short, defined, and can easily have a visual icon next to each rule showing the behavior. *Source: author created.*

whereas in another, it is not. It is recommended to use a word other than "respect." For example, instead of saying *respect the classroom instruments*, rephrased it as *carefully use two hands with the instruments*.

Consequences to rules should be clear, consistent, logical, and an opportunity to reflect and teach. Instead of using punishment, fear tactics, or authoritative strategies, music teachers should focus on the cause of the behavior and on replacement strategies. Remember, behavior is communication. Our goal is to replace the targeted behavior with something more appropriate and positive. It is important to note that consequences need to be consistent. Again, if students do not trust the system, then it will not work. The agreed-upon classroom rules and consequences need to apply to everyone.

Music teachers also need to consider the procedures developed in the classroom. Procedures are different from rules. **Procedures** are how we get from one activity or location to the next. Procedures must be taught early in the school year, and task analysis can help break them down into smaller steps. Music classrooms tend to have more procedures than others, so time needs to be taken to implement safe, appropriate procedures in the classroom or ensemble.

For example, visuals can again be paired to teach procedures. If the expectation is that students are transitioning from the classroom rug to go get Orff instruments, showcase a visual representation of step-by-step directions. In addition, break it down into small steps by having one student model first, then two students, and gradually build up.

Music teachers may also need to transition their classes to different locations within the school building. For example, they may need to pick up or drop their class from lunch or recess, especially in younger grades. Learning to walk safely and organized in the hallway is a procedure. Music teachers can use multisensory support to get students to transition safely. They can have visuals for walking in a line, putting hands on the stair rails, and walking to seats once in the room. Music teachers can also implement a song (e.g., I use "walking in a line" to the tune of "Farmer in the Dell"). Students have visual and auditory support as they move and complete the procedure. Keep in mind the age and developmental appropriateness of students (figure 7.2 shows an example of transitioning in the hallway procedure).

Music teachers also need to consider the **routines** planned in their classrooms. It is highly important that students can predict the order of the schedule. It is recommended to keep a consistent schedule for every music class. The only thing that changes is the actual repertoire used; however, the flow of activities would stay the same. If changes need to be made, notify students beforehand so they have time to process.

It is helpful to have a visual schedule posted in the classroom for ALL students to access. Younger students can use icons or pictures for each activity. You can also sing using musical phrasing to signal the beginning and when an activity is finished. In an ensemble, a schedule of which pieces will be worked on, which sections, and in which order should be posted. These will help support students who may struggle with anxiety,

1) Walking in a Line

2) Hands are on the Rail

3) Backpack on the Floor

4) Sitting in your Seat

Figure 7.2. This is a representation of a classroom procedure for transitioning early elementary music students from a different location in the building to the music room. The directions are shown to students while transitioning, and a song is sung to make it multisensory. Visuals can be paired with each step to help support students. *Source: author created.*

knowing what will happen and in which order (see figure 7.3 for an example of a middle-school music schedule).

Music teachers should also consider the pacing of certain activities. Every class will be different, as ALL students are different. Some classes can extend an activity, whereas others must move on quickly. Timers can be used to help students know how long an activity will last. As mentioned earlier, when creating a routine, consider energy levels. A higher-energy activity should be followed by a lower-energy activity to regulate the students.

Student empowerment is also important to suggest. When students have an active role in ALL aspects of the classroom, they will be more engaged, and targeted behaviors will decrease. For example, students can be responsible for monitoring their own behavior. A student can go around with a chart to ask their peers how and why they are doing so far. Afterward, each student can earn a point, resulting in something positive (figure 7.4 represents an example of how students are empowered to monitor their own behavior).

Some students need **redirection**. This can happen to any student, where they may just get off track. A gentle reminder can help support them in what they are supposed to be doing. Even more, a visual reminder can be of support, or sometimes prompting or cueing a student may be necessary. If a student gets off track, do not assume they are doing it on purpose and need a consequence. It is OK sometimes to need redirection. Keep things positive, get them where they need to be, and move on.

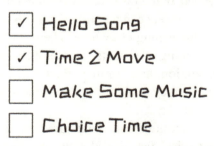

Figure 7.3. This is an example of a middle school classroom music schedule. The schedule stays the same for every class, and students can predict the order of activities. An icon such as a checkmark can show when each activity is finished, and visuals can be paired with each activity as well. *Source: author created.*

Are you being a **rock star**?

Yes   or   No

Why?

Soft Voice	Listen to Directions
Sit Down	Gentle Hands
Walk	Have Fun

Figure 7.4. This chart is part of a classroom procedure that a student would be responsible for using to ask the rest of the class how their behaviors are doing. The student asks if they are being rock stars, and the student can respond with yes or no. Then, they ask why, and the student has to respond with what behavior they are excelling at. This procedure is student-led and student-centered. Visual icons can be connected to each behavior to add another level of support. *Source: author created.*

INDIVIDUALIZED STUDENT SUPPORTS

Although basic classroom management strategies will work for most, some students may require additional individualized interventions; again, this population is usually around 15 percent. These students may need more support to help give them the tools to achieve success and find their best.

It is recommended that music teachers first reach out to the school community. Music teachers can mention the behaviors they are observing and see if they are happening elsewhere. The school community includes other teachers, teaching assistants, paraprofessionals, related service providers, administration, and families. Paraprofessionals can offer valid information here, as they may be with students in multiple locations throughout the school day.

It is essential to communicate with families, but keep in mind that if you discuss behavior, families already may be aware of challenges happening elsewhere. We want to create a partnership with families, so always keep communication positive rather than negative. Nevertheless, families can share any changes happening outside school that could be impacting classroom behavior.

Through communication, music teachers can determine whether the behavior occurs elsewhere or only in music. Moreover, they can learn which strategies other teachers may be using that are working and implement them as well. For individualized strategies, students must be able to generalize them in multiple locations.

Nevertheless, sometimes, the behavior occurs only in music. The music teacher now needs to figure out the behavior's function and how to replace it. To create a plan, collecting information or data on the behaviors is important. Data collection can help support a behavior plan in the music room. It is important to note that the behavior needs to be clearly defined. It should be something that the music teacher and/or staff observe, not what they assume.

One type of data collection is scatter plots. **Scatter plots** are charts where music teachers can tally when a clearly defined behavior occurs within the music classroom. Even more, if intensity levels vary, these can be added. If music teachers follow the same routine in each music class, they can use a scatter plot to analyze where and when a behavior occurs. The music teacher does not need to stop the class for formal documentation; just make a mark and keep going. It is important to note that multiple data days are required for comparison (see figure 7.5 for a scatter plot example).

Antecedent-behavior-consequence (ABC) charts are more detailed descriptions of a behavior occurring in class. An ABC chart will be filled out after the fact, or if paraprofessionals are watching the lesson, they can fill it out. The ABC chart will give more information than the scatter plot and needs multiple days of data to compare and contrast (sample ABC charts can easily be found online). Included in an ABC chart is

A (antecedent) = What happened before the behavior? What triggered it?
B (behavior) = What was the exact behavior that occurred?
C (consequence) = What happened after the behavior occurred?

Scatter plots show when and where the behavior occurs. ABC charts give a more detailed description of what happened immediately before and after the behavior. Once data collection is finished and analyzed, a

Student Name: Mohammad F. Date: 3/1/22
Targeted Behavior: Hitting Others

Activity	Number of Times	Intensity
Hello Song	✓ ✓ ✓	Tapping other peers during the song
Circle Time		
Vocal Warm-Up	✓	Hitting peers and self
Singing	✓ ✓	Hitting peers and self
Make Some Music		
Goodbye Song	✓	Tapping other peers during the song
Choice Time		

Figure 7.5. This is an example of a scatter plot used in my classroom, that a music teacher can fill out while teaching. Since the routine never changes, this will showcase more accurate data on where and when the behavior occurs. *Source: author created.*

behavior plan can be developed. Note: these are not formal behavior plans for a student's IEP. These are plans developed in the music classroom to help support and ensure student success. However, these plans should be communicated to the team if they work. Recommended student support strategies include

- first/then charts;
- token economy systems;
- checklists;
- individualized schedules;
- visual trackers;
- extra supports (fidget toys, sensory items, breaks);
- personal contracts;
- incorporating breaks into the schedule; and
- reward systems.

First/then charts are a primary way of replacing targeted behaviors and implementing a reinforcement. For example, if the behavior focused is sitting down, a chart can be created showing the expectation and something they are working for. The reinforcement should highly motivate the student, and they should have input. The reinforcement can change over time, as the student sometimes gets bored or wants

How Do We Create an Accessible, Strength-Based, Structured, and Predictable 135

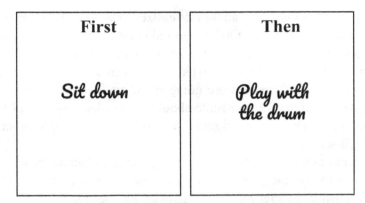

Figure 7.6. This is an example of a first/then chart. The behavior being worked on is getting the student to sit down. The student first sits, and then they can earn the drum which is motivating for this specific student. Visuals and icons can be added as well to make the chart more accessible. *Source: author created.*

change. Keep going. If this is the support they need to succeed, we must implement it (see figure 7.6 for an example of a first/then chart).

A **token economy system**, a technique used in applied behavioral analysis (ABA), is a more complex version of first/then. Students can work on multiple targeted behaviors and earn tokens throughout a set period. Each token is connected to the targeted behavior, with the student earning a motivating reinforcement at the end. Timers can help earn each token. If a student gets off task during a preset amount of time, the timer can be paused until the student is ready to continue.

It is important to note that as students earn tokens, we cannot take them away or threaten to. This is counterproductive to replacing behavior. ALL methods should focus on positive, preventative behavior and be encouraging. When we take away tokens, our students lose trust in the system, which will not work (see figure 7.7 for an example of a token economy system).

As mentioned in a previous chapter, checklists can be used to incorporate sequences that involve multiple steps. For example, if we teach students to raise their hands to share or ask a question, we can create a four-step checklist that they follow. This is an example of incorporating task analysis and can help students navigate the small, minute steps in between.

Some students may need an **individualized schedule**. These are schedules of the classroom routine or individualized steps they can follow and check off as complete. For students with anxiety, this can help them understand the lesson flow and what happens in what order. As talked about previously, if changes are going to be made, students need to be aware. An individualized schedule should be worded clearly and follow the basic classroom routine (figure 7.8 represents an example of an individualized schedule).

It is important to note that not ALL replacement behaviors will occur right away. Many times, a behavior gets worse before it gets better. This is what is called an **extinction burst**. Students may need to test the new system's boundaries and see whether the system is consistent. If a teacher is inconsistent with the plan, it will most likely not work. To be successful, ALL staff working in the music room must be on the same page regarding the strategy and implementation. Keeping the plan in place for at least two weeks is suggested. After that, if the behavior does not change, then revise the plan. But do not give up; plans take time.

It is important to note that music can help shape and replace behaviors. As touched on in the previous chapter, consider choosing repertoire that can be used as a vehicle to focus on targeted behaviors and incorporate

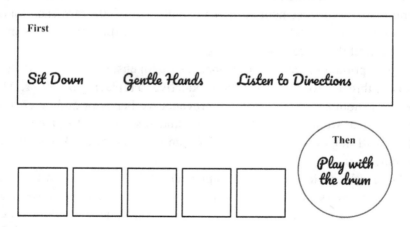

Figure 7.7. This is an example of a token economy system. The student is working on multiple behaviors and can earn a token for a set amount of time, then earn the motivating reinforcement. For example, if a student was focused on all three behaviors, they would earn a token for a set amount of time, which would go into each box. Visuals can be added as well. *Source: author created.*

Today, we are practicing the songs and dances for our spring show in the auditorium. I can sit in the audience with a quiet voice, hands down, and listen to directions.

Sit in the audience chair with a quiet voice and hands down.	
Dance to show song with a quiet voice and hands down.	
Sit in the audience chair with a quiet voice and hands down.	
Sing show song with a quiet voice and hands down.	
Choice time for 5 minutes with the laptop.	

Figure 7.8. This is an example of an individualized schedule. The student can check off each activity as it is completed. If changes need to be made to the schedule, they can be added to help support the student. *Source: author created.*

replacement strategies. Examples of how music can shape behavior include

- using music and repertoire students are interested in and identify with;
- incorporating music that is age and developmentally appropriate;
- using making music versus speaking to keep students engaged;
- incorporating multiple ways for students to engage;
- incorporate UDL and assistive technology;
- breaking content into smaller chunks to engage students;
- using music to teach replacement strategies;
- using music to build routines, transitions, and procedures;
- using musical conceptual teaching connections to build skills; and
- creating musical/rhythmic "codes" into the routine to keep the flow going.

It is important to note that some students may have outbursts or **meltdowns**. Within a class setting, sometimes we refer to this as a student going into crisis. A variety of reasons can cause this to occur. As every student is different, the behaviors will look different. Examples may include shutting down, crying, yelling, eloping, hitting, spitting, biting, pushing back, throwing materials, and more.

Following the protocol established with your school or district is crucial in this situation. It may even be that a person is designed to help support when this occurs. It is important to remember that when this happens, behavior is communication. Do not take things personally. Remain calm, try to redirect if possible, and follow established behavior plans. Music teachers and staff should never use punishment or fear in this situation. A meltdown, which is the only way they can communicate with us, might be out of a student's control. How can we humanly punish a student for trying to tell us something?

If it is possible to negotiate with the student during a meltdown, incorporating student choice can help. For example, assume that a student wants something and cannot get it, which causes an outburst. The teacher can then offer the student two or three other choices. In this situation, the student is empowered and can feel in control of the situation.

PERSONAL CONTEXT STORIES

Several years ago, I had a new student come into my program in seventh grade. He was not excited by or interested in anything to do with music. Despite trying to get to know him, creating a positive rapport, incorporating things he liked outside class, and developing behavioral plans, I could not find a way to engage him. At this time, we were getting ready for our upcoming musical theater performance. How could I force a seventh-grade student to go on stage and sing or dance without motivation? At this point, I was ready to let him sit it out.

I observed that outside class, he enjoyed and took ownership of helping support the early elementary students, and others looked up to him. I decided to incorporate his strength of being a natural leader and create the student role of assistant director for the show. After weeks of being given this responsibility, he began to take ownership of his role, which engaged him in his own unique way. Not only was he engaged, but it was also helpful for me in alleviating some of the responsibility. At one point, a fellow student soloist was absent, and this student volunteered to sing the song because he was the assistant director. I was shocked; he had never volunteered to sing or do anything similar.

At this point, I knew we had succeeded. Instead of forcing him to complete the work as I expected, I had to meet him where he was and redesign what success looked like for him. Music was never his favorite class, but I never got pushback or had behavioral issues afterward. He knew that a culture had been created where he felt empowered, recognized, relevant, and welcome.

A second example happened with a recent kindergarten music class. For the entire school year, this class has only had music in their actual classroom, as they were not ready to transition to the music room, which is located on a different floor and in a different part of the building. Every music class followed the same routine, like following a script, in the exact same way.

Toward the end of the school year, I decided it was time to transition them to the music room in preparation for the goal, which was that the following year, this was where music would take place. I discussed the plan with the room's staff, and we decided that the class would most likely only stay in the music room for a short time, as we expected chaos.

The students came to the room, and at first, they had no idea where they were. Some students started to get upset, and others wanted to touch ALL the new materials in the room. Instantly, I put on our music slides and our consistent routine. Within seconds, the students were engaged, even in a new location. Moreover, we were surprised that the students finished the entire lesson, and we could stay the whole class period.

This was due to having a consistent, predictable routine. The students knew exactly what would happen, in which order, and how we would do it. Even more, the language used was the same in every class. The fact that we were in a new location with many distractions did not matter. The structure was there, and we were able to make music.

CLOSING COMMENTS

We began this chapter by discussing Ms. Hodge's music class and Kimberly's needs. As we listed, Kimberly was most likely hypersensitive and experienced sensory overload during the musical activity. This transferred to her reactions, leading to her having to sit out of the musical activity.

This chapter focused more on the musical environment and ensuring that it is accessible for ALL students. We considered the way the music classroom looks and is organized and how students can have access to move around it. We then focused on students with sensory, medical, and physical needs. We ended by discussing behavior as a mode of communication and that ALL strategies should be used to replace behavior with something more appropriate.

As mentioned throughout this book, always focus on each student's strengths first. ALL students are capable of amazing things. Do not assume that a student cannot or will not. And when in doubt, ask. The student is the one who can tell us best what they need from us and how we can make it work.

So, what should Ms. Hodge do to help support Kimberly? What about her collaboration with the paraprofessional?

- Explain ahead of time about the music they will listen to.
- Have sensory materials available (e.g., noise-cancelling headphones).
- Ask Kimberly where she thinks she should sit to ensure success.
- Have a visual diagram available for Kimberly where she can choose or point to what she needed.
- Have a sensory cooldown area where Kimberly could have gone to self-regulate, with a timer set to give her a break.
- Allow Kimberly choice through the matter.
- Communicate with the paraprofessional to develop supportive and positive strategies.

REFLECTION QUESTIONS

1. What other ways can sensory input impact making music? How would you incorporate strategies to support ALL students?
2. How can you make your music classroom accessible to ALL? What would the location look like? What if you pushed into a different room?

3. What classroom rules have you developed for your students? Are they clearly defined for ALL?
4. What ways can you target specific behaviors that may be occurring, and what plans would you create? How would you implement them?

NOTES

1. Mary S. Adamek and Alice-Ann Darrow, *Music in Special Education*, first edition (American Music Therapy Association, 2005), 136.

2. Lee A. Wilkinson, *A Best Practice Guide to Assessment and Intervention for Autism Spectrum Disorder in Schools*, second edition (Jessica Kingsley, 2017), 182.

Chapter 8

Why?

ESSENTIAL QUESTIONS

1. How can music teachers implement the strategies to create an accessible music classroom for ALL?
2. Where can music teachers find additional resources, continuing education support, and professional networking opportunities to support ALL?

CORE VOCABULARY

Accessibility, unlearning, universal design for learning (UDL), multisensory learning, assistive technology, task analysis, conceptual learning, positive niche construction, developing independence, student empowerment, voice and choice, solid teamwork, belief that all can, professional learning communities (PLCs)

OPENING THOUGHTS: SELF-REFLECTION

One of my students' final assignments in the college class I teach is to complete a closing statement. The focus of this assignment is mainly on self-reflection and growth. My students can state what they learned, what challenged them, and how they grew as future music educators. As with the K–8 students I teach in a center-based special education program, I offer my college students multiple ways to complete the assignment (e.g., written statement, presentation, collage, etc.)—another example of UDL. For our sake, I want to go through the same process. However, because this is a book, you can answer the questions below however you feel.

The core focus of this text was to illustrate what an accessible music classroom looks like and how it can benefit everyone. For some, this may have been a journey of discovery filled with new content and fresh ideas. For others, it may have required a process of unlearning and a shift in perspective. And yet, some of you may have found points of disagreement with the content (I hope not). Regardless of your path, I am confident that each of you has experienced unique personal growth.

Think about the following:

1. What resonated with you the most from this text? What was your biggest takeaway?
2. How will it impact you and your students?
3. What are you still curious to know more about? What topics could have been included or gone into more detail?
4. How will you create a learning environment shaped by ALL student strengths and accessible to ALL?

As we add closure, everything discussed is from content I have presented in workshops and the college course I teach. This content will change with time (hopefully, this text will be revised to match those changes). Everything showcased here has been the focus of my career until now. I hope this work continues to evolve further to support the needs of ALL.

WHY ACCESSIBILITY FOR ALL?

As we begin to wrap up the focus of our work, we last need to consider *why*. Why is ALL this important? Why do we need to reconsider how we teach, who we teach, what we teach, and where we teach? And why do we need to come from a lens of ALL? We sometimes hear the phrase *if it works, why fix it*. It sounds easy to continue our educational pathway as it always was. But the problem, as you now know, is that it never worked. Most importantly, the parts that did work only worked for some, not ALL.

So here we are—accessibility for ALL. As our education system continuously shifts, we need to change with it for the sake of our students. Every student deserves an education tailored to their specific needs and meets them where they are. We face many obstacles when trying to engage our students right now. Instead of coming from the lens of *why fix it*, or *my way or the highway*, would it not be more accessible to ask *how we can make this work for you*? Even more, the way it works for you might work for others. It is not that hard, after ALL.

We used this text to consider the many aspects of what makes our classrooms accessible to ALL. Although some of our students have legal documentation that requires mandatory classroom changes, we need to get into a habit of teaching in a way that reaches ALL, allowing ALL students many ways to engage back.

We discussed the importance of unlearning. We have ALL been taught and raised in our own ways, and each pathway has shaped us to where we are. However, many techniques we have been taught are not fully accessible to ALL. This is not an insult to the fabulous teachers who helped prepare us. We know more now than we did then and are listening to many different intersections of voices to implement what is needed. ALL voices and opinions are necessary to steer us forward.

We then focused on the specific ideas that make our classrooms accessible. Throughout this book, we used universal design for learning (UDL) as the pillar of our focus. How many ways can we teach music to our students? And how many ways can we allow our students to respond? We highlighted the fact that the strategies used for the students who have the most needs will benefit ALL. Although this work focused on students with disabilities, every student benefits from teaching in an accessible style.

We considered multisensory learning and connected it directly to UDL. When we present our content with multiple access points, everyone has a way. We considered visual, auditory, kinesthetic, and tactile. We spent an entire chapter discussing various aspects of the musical curriculum and how this connects to it.

We discussed assistive technology and how it can easily be used to give more students access to high-quality, standards-based music. Some assistive technology will be added to a student's IEP. Nevertheless, many additional musical and assistive technology types can be implemented to make music.

We talked about the importance of task analysis or breaking things down. Throughout this book, we examined several examples of how task analysis was used in action. It is vital for ALL to break things down. ALL our brains are different and decode and process in their own unique ways. When we present information in sequential and orderly steps, things will make more sense for ALL.

We also discussed the importance of conceptual learning. When we connect to things our students are familiar with and use them as a tool in our classrooms, abstract and new concepts will be easier to teach. Get familiar with your students and what they already know and use that as a tool. Consider aspects of their communities, locations, interests, nature, and so forth. It will only make teaching and learning more relatable for ALL.

We also touched on the aspects of a strength-based model, which will only enhance accessibility for ALL. We connected to Thomas Armstrong's positive niche construction. To summarize, it is important that we create an environment shaped around the individual strengths of ALL students. We should not force our students to fit a predesigned mold; this will only benefit some, not ALL.

Several times, we have highlighted the development of independence and student empowerment. We need to get rid of the mind-set that we are the teachers, they are the students, and they will do what we command. Instead, let us create a community where everyone feels a sense of worth and ownership. As you have seen, this can benefit self-esteem, emotions, engagement, and behavior. Let students feel proud of the work they do and be part of your program's culture.

We mentioned the importance of student voice and choice. We need their input, ideas, and opinions to shape where we must go. We can only assume if we do not know—and I am sure you know what it means to assume. When in doubt, ask. It is pretty straightforward. Especially regarding students with disabilities, ask them what they need and how we can help. Their voices, not our egos, are the ones that truly matter in the end.

We touched on the importance of solid teamwork. We cannot do this alone. Create a positive rapport with your school community and families. If paraprofessionals work in your classroom, developing a positive relationship with them is critical. This is also on us. We need to find ways to get them on our side for the benefit of our students. Let them feel part of the team and that their voice is heard.

Most importantly, do you believe that ALL students can? You may have your own biases that impact your opinions in the classroom but try to unlearn them and connect them to where your students are coming from. Consider other ways you can approach teaching and see if they work. Consider adjusting your mind-set so that it is not that our students cannot, but that it is the barrier preventing them from achieving success.

WHAT DOES THIS LOOK LIKE FOR YOU?

I think it is safe to say that we have officially added enough content. But now, what do we do with this? Remember, many of the examples showcased are from my classroom or examples of how I have used these practices. It will look different for you. You need to consider your students' age and developmental skills, what type of music program you are teaching, who your students are, and how you can connect with them.

A considerable part of creating an accessible music classroom for ALL is self-reflection. We need to take time to consider whether we are reaching ALL students. Consider the materials, repertoire, strategies, pacing, environment, and more. As we go through this process, we will make mistakes—we are human. However, we must think about what worked, what did not, and what changes need to be made.

We tend to get into a habit of teaching a lesson and reteaching it the same way the following year. But the students we have the following year will be different. We need to reflect on how we are connecting with them. We must also consider whether the original lesson was accessible in ALL aspects. Allow self-reflection to become part of your regular teaching practice and be open to your own constructive feedback to enhance your teaching.

Ask your students for their opinions and voices as well. Throughout the school year, you can create several simple surveys or forms for students to fill out and give feedback. You can ask them if they feel the work is connecting to them, accessible, challenging, or too easy, and if they could change one thing, what would it be? This feedback is hugely relevant and essential. You can also contact family and community members who are doing the same. Their voices are the ones that should shape your changes.

When you consider implementing changes to your teaching practice to make it more accessible, consider where to begin. When I present a workshop, I often hear feedback that *I don't know where to start*. That is totally understandable. When I present a session, you see fifteen years of progress in a one-hour workshop—not something developed overnight.

Start with just one aspect that resonates with you. This could be adding more visuals to your curriculum and content or breaking your lessons into smaller segments. Consider your students, their needs, and what aspect would be easier to start with. This may be harder for seasoned teachers because they might be set in their ways. So, start simple and gradually add more.

LIFELONG LEARNING AND GROWTH OPPORTUNITIES

Part of the self-reflection process is recognizing that we are also lifelong learners. As teachers, we need to acknowledge that the field of education changes and shifts constantly, and we need to be part of that process. As music educators, if we are focused on educational research we often only consider what is happening in the general education discourse. Nevertheless, we must be part of the change and consider what this looks like in our music classrooms and ensembles.

Music teachers should be part of **professional learning communities (PLCs)** to help create a network to navigate the changes and how they apply to music. PLCs can exist within a school setting, department, district, or zone, locally, statewide, nationally, or internationally. Check with your state or local music education organizations to see what PLCs are available.

Music teachers should also be part of local and state music education organizations. These may provide professional development, access to journals, networking, community, and student performance opportunities. It is recommended that you find which local and state chapters are located near you. Even more, become active with them. Suggest which resources you need to help facilitate the discussion to get them. For example, if you need more professional development regarding accessible music education, then inquire about getting clinicians to present.

For example, I am a member and the neurodiversity and accessibility state chair for the New York State School Music Association (NYSSMA®). NYSSMA® is the largest state affiliate in the nation and has been and remains a leading and influential organization. The organization has an annual conference, where several workshops focus on accessible and inclusive music education. The organization's journal, *School Music News*, provides publications throughout the school year. Student opportunities are provided throughout New York several times a year.

Lastly, consider the many types of communities and organizations that exist. Many of these can benefit you as music educators, and others may help your students. For example, the Berklee Institute for Accessible Arts Education (BIAAE)[1] offers multiple aspects that can benefit ALL, from hybrid lessons for ALL students to a hybrid conference on accessible arts education.

The Office of Accessibility and VSA at the Kennedy Center[2] provides multiple professional development opportunities and student opportunities through its programs. The Division of Visual and Performing Arts Education with the Council for Exceptional Children (CEC)[3] offers resources and publications to support music teachers.

WHAT HAPPENS NEXT?

Now that we are literally at the end, it is your turn to take ALL this new knowledge and implement it. Not only that but share it. We will only continue to progress and grow if we share our successes. If we remain isolated from our community and network, we risk taking longer to get where we need to go, ultimately impacting our students.

Think about the potential partnerships you can forge to impact your students and community positively. Better yet, consider creating your own resources or organization to enhance accessibility for ALL. For those with networking or creative skills, we need more accessible resources for our students. Whether establishing a performance studio for neurodivergent students or publishing a book of accessible resources, these initiatives would be a game-changer for our community.

Think about the opportunities you can create for your students to become part of our communities. Whether through collaborations with cultural institutions or organizations or by making personal connections, ALL students would benefit from chances to showcase their talents in the real world. We can make this happen; we just need to take the initiative.

I hope this book is a helpful resource for you. As you can tell, I am passionate about what I do and believe in ALL my students. I hope this makes a connection with you and that you consider what this would look like for you. It is time we rethink our profession and consider how we can make an accessible music classroom for ALL.

NOTES

1. "Berklee Institute for Accessible Arts Education," Berklee College of Music, accessed August 25, 2024, https://college.berklee.edu/BIAAE.

2. "Access/VSA," Kennedy Center, accessed August 25, 2024, https://www.kennedy-center.org/education/vsa/.

3. "Division of Visual and Performing Arts Education," Council for Exceptional Children, accessed August 25, 2024, https://darts.exceptionalchildren.org/.

Appendix A
Sample Lesson Activities

Musical Activity: "Kalan Nege," performed by Issa Bagayogo

Age Range: General Music, Grades 1–2

Accessible Learning Objective: Using visual supports, students will be able to use movement, body percussion, rhythm syllables, and/or instruments to perform the accompaniment to "Kalan Nege" with 85 percent accuracy by the end of the class period.

Task Analysis: First, have students listen to the audio track with a visualizer and icons to represent the way the music is organized. Then, have students describe what they noticed in the music (e.g., they can share or discuss, point to the pictures, use movement or gestures, etc.). Next, have students use the Go and Stop icons to move with the music—they can dance, clap, or wave their arms during Go and then freeze during Stop. Then, have students perform an accompaniment using body percussion, instruments, movement, or technology to make a sound when they see Go and a quiet sound when they see Stop. Next, connect Go and Stop to a green quarter note and a red quarter rest. Go through the same process using a note and a rest instead of Go and Stop. Have students perform the accompaniment as they choose now using a note and a rest (see figures A1 and A2 for examples).

Musical Activity: "Billie Jean," performed by Michael Jackson

Age Range: General Music, Grades 4–6

Accessible Learning Objective: Using visual supports, students will be able to use instruments, body percussion, and/or rhythm syllables individually or in small groups to perform the accompaniment to "Billie Jean,"

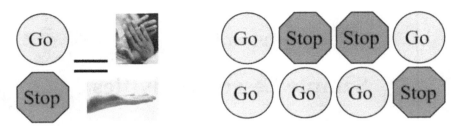

Figure A1. The left image shows how to teach Go to clap hands, while Stop means to make a quiet sound. The right image shows how Go and Stop can be a precursor to literacy, and students can perform it however they choose. *Source: author created using non-copyrighted images from Pexels.*

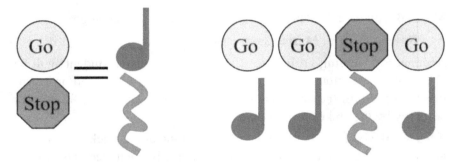

Figure A2. The left image shows how Go can be connected to a green quarter note, and Stop can be connected to a red quarter rest. The music teacher can explain that this is another way of showing Go and Stop. The right image is an example of connecting to music literacy and presenting the information differently. *Source: author created.*

combining quarter notes, eighth notes, and quarter rests with 85 percent accuracy by the end of the class period.

Task Analysis: Introduce the music, artist, background, and historical and cultural context of the song. Next, listen to the music and see how many ways students can find the steady beat. The teacher can have a color-coded slide with the numbers 1–4 and visuals of different movements that can be done with the body to show each beat (e.g., clap, stomp, wave, dab, floss). Start the music, begin counting to four, and model how to find the number four in multiple ways (e.g., counting, pointing, tapping, moving). Next, showcase the color-coded music notation (include icons or Go and Stop if necessary). Last, provide multiple ways for students to demonstrate (body percussion, rhythm syllables, movement, instruments, or technology; see figures A3, A4, and A5 for examples).

Sample Lesson Activities   153

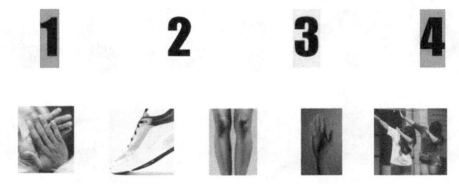

Figure A3. This image shows the multiple ways we can track and show the steady beat. Students can count the numbers out loud, point to them, choose from the different movement options presented (e.g., clap hands, stomp feet, tap knees, wave arms, dab), or devise their own way. This can be applied to each repertoire example to add predictability to the routine. *Source: author created using non-copyrighted images from Pexels.*

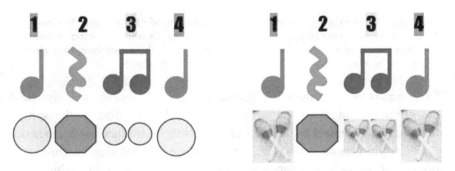

Figure A4. The left image shows the rhythmic accompaniment, connected to Go and Stop icons, using various sizes. The right image goes through the same process, using pictures of instruments and adjusting the size to represent rhythm. *Source: author created using non-copyrighted images from Pexels.*

Musical Activity: "You're My Best Friend," performed by Queen

Age Range: General Music, Grades 7–8

Accessible Learning Objective: With visual supports, students will be able to use instruments, movement, solfège, or technology individually or in small groups to perform the accompaniment to "You're My Best Friend," combining the pitches Do, Fa, and Sol with 85 percent accuracy by the end of the class period.

Figure A5. The image represents full accompaniment of "Billie Jean." Students can choose a part they want to perform by telling, pointing, or using the letter representation. They can then perform their accompaniment with the music how they choose.
Source: author created using non-copyrighted images from Pexels.

Task Analysis: Introduce the music, artist, background, and historical and cultural context of the song. Go even deeper, discuss the song's meaning, and connect to the idea of friendship. Introduce the pitches do, fa, and sol in various ways (e.g., singing, Curwen hand signs, technology, movement, musical instruments). Practice several examples using these three pitches in multiple different ways. Last, have students perform the accompaniment to "You're My Best Friend" however they choose (see figure A6 for an example).

Musical Activity: Vocal Warm-Up

Age Range: General Music, Grades 4–8

Accessible Learning Objective: With visual supports, students will be able to use their voices, bodies, or assistive technology to represent different sounds in a vocal warm-up with 85 percent accuracy by the end of the class period.

Task Analysis: Introduce the three parts of the vocal warm-up. First, model how long our voices are on the sound *ahh*. Students can use their

Sample Lesson Activities 155

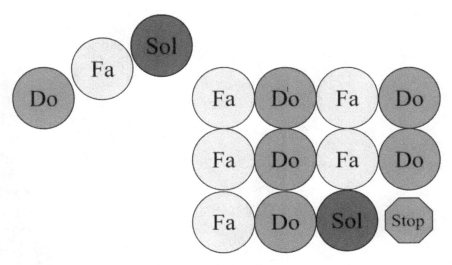

Figure A6. The left image introduces the Do (red), Fa (green), and Sol (blue) pitches using colors and solfège. The right image represents the accompaniment to the refrain to "You're My Best Friend." Students can perform it on classroom instruments, sing, use Curwen hand signs, or use technology. *Source: author created.*

voice, their bodies to trace it, their fingers to touch it on a printed sheet with Velcro, or Chrome Music Lab to create a visual representation. Next, model how our voices can go high and low using the same sound. Students can use their voices and arms to trace the contour or use assistive technology. Then, have students sing a scale in solfège with a backing track. Students can sing the solfège sounds, use Curwen hand signs, play on an instrument, or use assistive technology. Last, a student volunteer can independently use a script to lead the vocal warm-up (see figure A7 for an example).

Musical Activity: "Day Is Done," performed by Peter, Paul and Mary

Age Range: General Music, Grades 1–2

Accessible Learning Objective: Individually or in small groups, students will be able to either sing, use gestures or movements, and/or point to demonstrate lyrical understanding of the song "Day Is Done" with 85 percent accuracy by the end of the class period.

Task Analysis: After the song "Day Is Done" is introduced, teach the refrain by rote. For each line, one keyword will be chosen and presented

156 · *Appendix A*

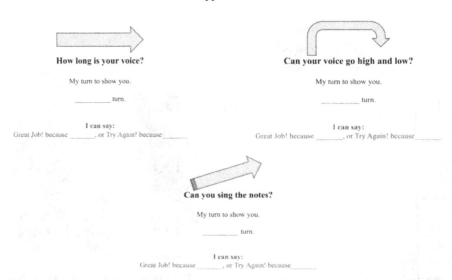

Figure A7. The image represents the script version of the vocal warm-up that a student leader would use to model each example and then ask peers to demonstrate. *Source: author created.*

with a gesture and a bolded and highlighted version. A visual will also be paired with each keyword. Gradually, as the refrain is put together, students can sing, use the gestures, point to the visuals, or use a recordable talking button to follow along. During the verse to the song, students can use dancing scarves to move along to follow the overall form of the music (figure A8 shows an example of this in action).

Musical Activity: "It's OK," performed by Imagine Dragons

Age Range: General Music, Grades 8–9

Accessible Learning Objective: Individually or in small groups, students will be able to either sing, use gestures or movements, and/or point to demonstrate lyrical understanding of the song "It's OK" with 85 percent accuracy by the end of the class period.

Task Analysis: The music teacher would follow a strategy like "Day Is Done." The visuals look different in this example because this is designed for older students, and age appropriateness needs to be considered. After the song is taught, students have multiple ways to perform it back. Students can sing, use gestures, point, or use technology. Gradually, the

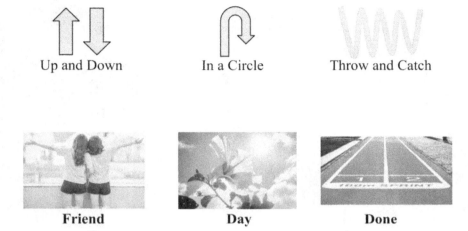

Figure A8. The image showcases a visual representation of what the refrain would look like in a multisensory way. The top part of the song showcases the different moves that students could do with the dancing scarves during the verse. The bottom part shows key text from the refrain using words, images, gestures, and assistive technology. *Source: author created using non-copyrighted images from Pexels.*

music teacher can use a Go and Stop sign to teach the song by rote and have students perform it as a small ensemble (see figure A9 for an example of the visual representation).

Musical Activity: "Raiders of the Lost Ark," from *Raiders of the Lost Ark*

Age Range: General Music, Grades 4–6

Accessible Learning Objective: Using movement and visual supports, individually and/or in small groups, students will be able to identify and describe the rondo form sections in the "Raiders of the Lost Ark" theme with 85 percent accuracy by the end of the class period.

Task Analysis: First, introduce the movie, character, and story to give context to the music. Connections can be made to the "Star Wars Theme" as well. Use a visual map and a parachute or stretchy band, and have students follow the different movements at each section. After they perform, have students work together to figure out the letter form of the music, which is rondo form. Last, students can create their own rondo composition using instruments, sound effects, movement, technology, or visuals (see figure A10 for the visual representation of the form).

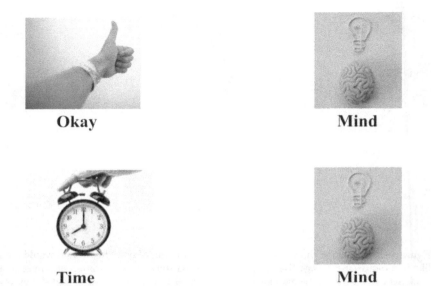

Figure A9. The image showcases a visual representation of what the refrain would look like in a multisensory way. *Source: author created using non-copyrighted images from Pexels.*

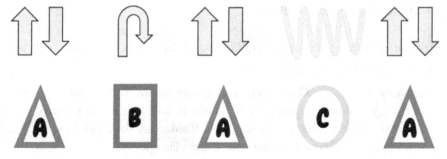

Figure A10. The image represents the form and movements that accompany the "Raiders of the Lost Ark" theme. During the A section, students move their parachute or stretchy band up and down. During the B section, students spin in a circle. During the C section, students make fast waves. The form letters are represented in multiple ways, using color, shapes, and letters. *Source: author created.*

Sample Lesson Activities 159

Musical Activity: "Dance the Night," performed by Dua Lipa

Age Range: General Music, Grades 7–8

Accessible Learning Objective: Using visual supports, students will be able to perform the dance to the song "Dance the Night" as an entire ensemble with 85 percent accuracy by the end of the class period.

Task Analysis: First, give context to the song and explain that it is from the 2023 motion picture *Barbie*. Have a volunteer model the dance with the visuals on the board. Provide a script where students can converse with peers to discuss their observations. Have students select a dancing spot and place it on the floor. Teach the dance to the song with the visuals provided. Gradually, put the dance together with the music (see figure A11 for this in action).

Musical Activity: "Hallelujah," originally performed by Leonard Cohen

Age Range: String Orchestra, Grades 9–10

Accessible Learning Objective: Using color-coded musical notation and adapted string instruments, students will be able to perform the song

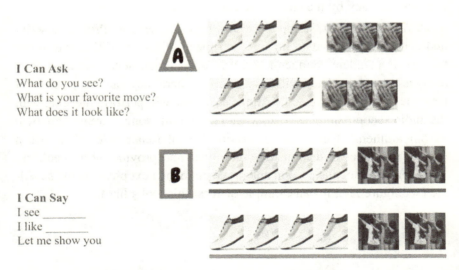

Figure A11. The left image showcases a script a student leader can use to ask peers questions about the dance. The colors green (I Can Ask text) and red (I Can Say text) connect to Go and Stop. The right image showcases a visual map of the dance. Each picture represents one move, with the color-coded lines (yellow, green, blue, and red) underneath showcasing which direction students will be moving in. *Source:* author created using non-copyrighted images from Pexels.

160 *Appendix A*

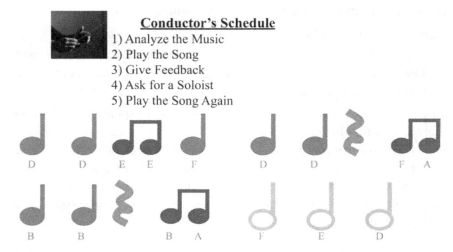

Figure A12. **The top image showcases the conductor's schedule for each piece of music. The bottom image showcases a sample of the color-coded musical notation of "Hallelujah," which has been adapted to meet the students' level.** *Source: author created using non-copyrighted images from Pexels.*

"Hallelujah" combining quarter notes, eighth notes, and half notes with 85 percent accuracy by the end of the class period.

Task Analysis: First, set up and warm up the ensemble. Provide a script and schedule for what to do for each piece of music. Either the music teacher or a student conductor will follow the music schedule. First, they analyze the music. They will have a script where they can ask peers what they see in the sheet music. Next, the ensemble will perform the song with the audio accompaniment (e.g., when I taught this song, I created my own accompaniment). Next, provide feedback to the ensemble. Then, ask a student volunteer to demonstrate the music and provide more feedback. Last, perform the music again and move on to the next piece on the schedule (see figure A12 for an example of what this looks like).

Appendix B

Suggested Resources

FEDERAL LAWS AND INFORMATION

Americans with Disabilities Act (ADA), 1990
https://www.ada.gov/

Every Student Succeeds Act (ESSA), 2015
https://www.ed.gov/essa?src=ft

Individuals with Disabilities Education Act (IDEA), 1997
https://sites.ed.gov/idea

Jacob K. Javits Gifted and Talented Students Education Act, 1988
https://oese.ed.gov/offices/office-of-discretionary-grants-support-services/well-rounded-education-programs/jacob-k-javits-gifted-and-talented-students-education-program/

National Association for Music Education The Every Student Succeeds Act https://nafme.org/wp-content/uploads/2023/04/ESSA-In-Plain-EnglishFINAL-2-2016.pdf

Our Nation's English Learners
https://www2.ed.gov/datastory/el-characteristics/index.html

ORGANIZATIONS, PROFESSIONAL DEVELOPMENT, AND RESOURCES

Access/VSA The Kennedy Center
https://www.kennedy-center.org/education/vsa/

Berklee Institute of Accessible Arts Education (BIAAE)
https://college.berklee.edu/BIAAE

Center for Applied Special Technology (CAST)
https://www.cast.org/

Collaborative for Academic, Social, and Emotional Learning (CASEL)
https://casel.org/

Council for Exceptional Children (CEC)
https://exceptionalchildren.org/

Council for Exceptional Children Division of Visual and Performing Arts Education (DARTS)
https://darts.exceptionalchildren.org/

ISME Special Music Education & Music Therapy
https://www.isme-commissions.org/special-education.html

National Association for Music Education (NAfME)
https://nafme.org/

National Association for Music Education Accessible Music Education Special Research Interest Group (SRIG)
https://sites.google.com/view/exceptionalities-srig

West Music
https://www.westmusic.com/

ASSISTIVE MUSICAL TECHNOLOGY

Artiphon
https://artiphon.com/

Beamz
https://beamzinteractive.com/

Clarion
https://www.openupmusic.org/clarion

EyeHarp
https://eyeharp.org/

Figurenotes
https://figurenotes.org/

Jamboxx
https://www.jamboxx.com/

Launchpad X
https://us.novationmusic.com/products/launchpad-x

Makey Makey®
https://makeymakey.com/

Orba 2
https://artiphon.com/products/orba2

Soundbeam
https://www.soundbeam.co.uk/

APPLICATIONS AND WEBSITES

BeatBlocks
https://beatblocks.app/

Chrome Music Lab
https://musiclab.chromeexperiments.com/Experiments

Creatability Experiments by Google
https://experiments.withgoogle.com/collection/creatability

GarageBand
https://www.apple.com/mac/garageband/

Incredibox
https://www.incredibox.com/

Keezy
https://keezy.net/

Paint Melody
https://apps.apple.com/us/app/paint-melody-draw-music/id680278617

ThumbJam
https://thumbjam.com/

ADDITIONAL TEXTS FOR ACCESSIBLE MUSIC EDUCATION

Adamek, M. S., and A. Darrow. *Music in Special Education*, third edition. American Music Therapy Association, 2018.

Blair, D. V., and K. A. McCord. *Exceptional Music Pedagogy for Children with Exceptionalities* (International Perspectives). Oxford University Press, 2016.

Edgar, S. N. *Music Education and Social Emotional Learning: The Hear of Teaching Music*. GIA Publications, 2017.

Hammel, A. M., R. Y. Hickox, and R. M. Hourigan. *Winding It Back: Teaching to Individual Differences in Music Classroom and Ensemble Settings*. Oxford University Press, 2016.

Hammel, A. M., and R. M. Hourigan. *Teaching Music to Students with Autism*, second edition. Oxford University Press, 2020.

———. *Teaching Music to Students with Special Needs: A Label-Free Approach*, second edition. Oxford University Press, 2017.

Hansen, D., E. Bernstorf, and G. M. Stuber. *The Music and Literacy Connection*. National Association for Music Education, 2004.

Jellison, J. A. *Including Everyone: Creating Music Classrooms Where All Children Learn*. Oxford University Press, 2015.

McPherson, G. E., and G. F. Welch. *Special Needs, Community Music, and Adult Learning (An Oxford Handbook of Music Education*, volume 4. Oxford University Press, 2018.

MENC: The National Association for Music Education. *Spotlight on Making Music with Special Learners: Selected Articles from State MEA Journals* (Spotlight Series). R&L Education, 2004.

Sobol, E. S. *An Attitude and Approach for Teaching Music to Special Learners*, third edition. Rowman & Littlefield in partnership with the National Association for Music Education, 2017.

OTHER PUBLICATIONS AS AUTHOR

Wagner, B. "Engaging All Learners: Tools and Techniques to Reach Different Types of Learners in the Music Classroom." *School Music News*. New York State School Music Association, 2015.

———. "Engaging All Types of Learners in the Music Classroom." *Music in a Minuet*. National Association for Music Education, 2017.

———. "Making Connections for Special Learners: Using Repertoire to Enhance Lifelong Learning." *School Music News*. New York State School Music Association, 2016.

———. "Using a Differentiated Rhythmic and Melodic Notation System for Special Learners in All Musical Settings." *Tempo*. New Jersey Music Educators Association, 2017.

———. "Using Repertoire to Enhance Lifelong Learning." *Music in a Minuet*. National Association for Music Education, 2016.

Wagner-Yeung, B. "Behavioral Supports for Students with Special Needs in Musical Environments." *Music in a Minuet*. National Association for Music Education, 2018.

———. "Distance Learning for Special Learners in the Music Classroom." *Music in a Minuet*. National Association for Music Education, 2020.

———. "Inclusive Strategies for Students with ASD in the Music Room." *Music ConstructED*. West Music, 2022.

———. "Let's Make Music! Engaging Students with Autism Spectrum Disorders in the K–8 General Music Classroom." *Music ConstructED*. West Music, 2020.

———. "Neurodiversity in the Music Classroom: Using the Strengths of All Students during In-Person and Remote Learning." *School Music News*. New York State School Music Association, 2021.

———. "Related Service Providers in the Music Classroom." *DARTS Newsletter*. Council for Exceptional Children, 2019.

———. "Teaching Lessons to Children with Special Needs." *Music in a Minuet*. National Association for Music Education, 2018.

———. "What's in a Label? An Inclusive Person-First & Strength-Based Approach." *School Music News*. New York State School Music Association, 2023.

Index

504 accommodation plan, 22, 50–51, 54
AAC. *See* augmentative and alternative communication
ABA. *See* applied behavioral analysis
ABC charts. *See* data collection; antecedent–behavior–consequence
ableism, 40; ableist, 40–41
access, 5–6, 63, 145
accessible learning objectives, 48–49
Accessible Music Education Special Research Interest Group, 55
accommodations, 50–51
ADA. *See* Americans with Disabilities Act of 1990
Adamek, Mary S., 126
adaptations, 50–51, 54
administrators, 34
age and developmentally appropriate, 63–64, 93
all, 7, 13–14, 64, 144–145
American Psychological Association (APA), 25, 41; bias-free language, 25; inclusive language guide, 41
American Speech-Language-Hearing Association (ASHA): language and communication, 91; augmentative and alternative communication (AAC), 101
Americans with Disabilities Act of 1990 (ADA), 20

anxiety, 78, 130–131, 136
APA. *See* American Psychological Association
applied behavioral analysis (ABA), 135
Armstrong, Thomas, 15, 41, 146; positive niche construction, 41, 146
ASHA. *See* American Speech-Language-Hearing Association
assistive technology, 54, 122, 124, 145
augmentative and alternative communication (AAC), 101–102

backward planning, 47
barriers, 6, 8
behavior, 121, 125–127, 129, 132–133, 136, 138; attention seeking, 126; classroom management, 128; classroom rules, 128; consequences, 129; escape, 126; extinction burst, 136; extinguish, 127; learned helplessness, 125; meltdowns, 137; replace, 127, 136
behavioral intervention plan (BIP), 22, 127
belief that all can, 42, 147
belonging, 6–7
Berklee Institute of Accessible Arts Education (BIAAE), 5, 7, 149
Bernard, Rhoda, 5, 52

BIAAE. *See* Berklee Institute of Accessible Arts Education
bias, 41–42
blues music, 110
BIP. *See* behavioral intervention plan
Boston University: *inequality, equality, equity, justice*, 7
Brackett, Marc, 106
Braille music, 122

CAST. *See* Center for Applied Special Technology
CASEL. *See* Collaborative for Academic, Social, and Emotional Learning
CDC. *See* Centers for Disease Control and Prevention
CEC. *See* Division of Visual and Performing Arts Education with the Council for Exceptional Children
Center for Applied Special Technology (CAST), 52
Centers for Disease Control and Prevention (CDC), 16, 105–106
Chalkbeat New York, 106
checklists, 74–75, 135
classroom environment, 119–120, 122, 125
classroom teachers, 34
cochlear implants, 121
Collaborative for Academic, Social, and Emotional Learning (CASEL), 105
cognition, 93–95; input, 94; output, 94; retention, 94
Cokley, Rebecca, 7
color-coding, 65–66
communication, 97–98, 121, 125
composition, 82–83
conceptual learning, 57–58, 65–66, 146
COVID–19, 5, 19, 23
Crenshaw, Kimberlé, 24

Darrow, Alice-Ann, 126

data collection, 133; antecedent-behavior-consequence (ABC) charts, 133; scatter plots, 133
developing independence, 42, 55, 81, 111, 146
Diagnostic and Statistical Manual of Mental Disorders (DSM–V), 19
disabilities, 16, 37, 39; identity-first language (IFL), 39; person-first language (PFL), 39; non-apparent disabilities, 17, 51; visible disabilities, 16
disability models, 37–38; charity model, 37; medical model, 37; neurodiversity affirming model, 38; social model, 37
Division of Visual and Performing Arts Education with the Council for Exceptional Children (CEC), 149
DSM–V. *See* Diagnostic and Statistical Manual of Mental Disorders

Early Start Denver Model (EDSM), 112
echolalia, 98; delayed echolalia, 98; immediate echolalia, 98
EDSM. *See* Early Start Denver Model
EL. *See* English learners
emotional intelligence, 106
emotional regulation, 104–106
engage, 15, 48–49, 52–53
English learners (EL), 24
ensembles, 71, 78
equity, 4, 63
ESSA. *See* Every Student Succeeds Act of 2015
Every Student Succeeds Act of 2015 (ESSA), 20, 33
exclusion, 6

family and community members, 16, 20, 36, 132–133, 146
Family Education Rights and Privacy Act (FERPA), 22

Index

FAPE. *See* free and appropriate public education
FBA. *See* formal behavioral analysis
FERPA. *See* Family Education Rights and Privacy Act
Feuerstein, Reuven, 93–94
Filomen M. D'Agostino Greenberg Music School, 122
first/then charts, 134
FM system, 122
formal behavioral analysis (FBA), 22

generalization, 51, 65, 90
gifted and talented, 23
Glasgow, David, 6
Gobir, Nimah, 52
Google: Chrome Music Lab, 70, 76, 122, 155; Creatability through Experiments, 55, 72, 77, 85
Grimsby, Rachel, 35
Guild for Human Services, 98

Hammel, Alice, 23, 93–94
hearing aids, 122
higher support needs, 18, 39
Hourigan, Ryan M., 23, 93–94

iconic images, 65
IDEA. *See* Individuals with Disabilities Education Act
IEP. *See* individualized education program
IFL. *See* language; identity–first language
implicit bias, 41
inclusion: 42 U.S. Code § 15002, 6
individualized education program (IEP), 21–22, 34, 50–51, 54, 123
individualized schedule, 136
Individuals with Disabilities Education Act (IDEA), 17, 19, 93, 105; free and appropriate education (FAPE), 20; least restrictive environment, 20; parent involvement, 20; procedural due process, 20; thirteen disability categories, 17, 105; zero reject, 19
intersectionality, 24

Jacob K. Javits Gifted and Talented Students Education Program, 23
JARS. *See* joint activity routines
Jellison, Judith A., 32
joint activity routines (JARS), 112

Kennedy Center. *See* Office of Accessibility and VSA at The Kennedy Center

Ladau, Emily, 38, 40
language, 38, 97–98, 121; expressive language, 97; non-speakers, 39, 98; receptive language, 97
learning objectives, 47–48, 93
LGBTQIA2S+ community, 24
lifelong learning, 89–92, 148
listening maps, 75

Mager, Robert F., 47
making connections, 92–93
masking, 17
medical or physical needs, 123, 125
mental health, 23, 105
Middleton, Ellie, 6, 17, 40
modifications, 50–51
mood meter, 107
music benefits, *33*, 89
music education, 32; high-quality music education, 32, 89, 91; standards-based music education, 33, 47
musical instruments, 71–74
musical listening, 75, 77
music literacy, 64–65, 67, 83–84
musical theatre, 78–79
multisensory learning, 53, 122, 145

NAfME. *See* National Association for Music Education

National Association for Music Education (NAfME), 33, 36, 55
National Core Arts Standards, 15, 33, 48, 91–92; anchor standard #11, 92
NeuroClastic, 98
neurodiversity, 14–15; neurodivergence, 15; neurodivergent, 15; neurotypical, 15
New York City Blueprint for the Arts in Music, 33
New York State Education Department, 50
New York State School Music Association (NYSSMA®), 149
nondiscriminatory evaluation, 20
Novak, Katie, 37, 52
NYSSMA®. *See* New York State School Music Association

Office of Accessibility and VSA at The Kennedy Center, 149
Office of Elementary and Secondary Education. *See* Jacob K. Javits Gifted and Talented Students Education Program
Office of Special Education and Rehabilitative Services, 19
outside organizations and resources, 36

pacing, 131
paraprofessionals, 35–36, 42, 123, 132, 146–147
PBIS. *See* positive behavioral intervention support
PBL. *See* project based learning
PEC symbols. *See* picture exchange system
PFL. *See* language; person-first language
picture exchange system (PEC symbols), 102
planned ignoring, 126
planning and goals, 47

PLCs. *See* professional learning communities
Posey, Allison, 37
positive behavioral intervention support (PBIS), 127
procedures, 129
professional learning communities (PLCs), 148
project based learning (PBL), 112

Ravishankar, Rakshitha A., 38–39
redirection, 131
related services, 21
related service providers, 34–35; occupational therapists, 73, 120, 122; physical therapists, 73, 123; speech language pathologists (SLP's), 98–99, 102–103
repertoire, 92–93
restrictive and repetitive behaviors, 121
routines, 104, 130

Sacks, Oliver, 32
School Music News, 149
scripts, 100–101, 107
SEL. *See* social emotional learning
self-esteem, 109
self-reflection, 147–148
sensory needs, 120, 125; hypersensitive, 120–121; hyposensitive, 121; sensory materials, 122
sensory overload, 121
shaping, 4, 36, 42, 126–127, 145
Singer, Judith, 14
singing, 68, 71
six domains, 23
SLP's. *See* related service providers; speech language pathologists
Sobol, Elise S., 48, 57, 92, 94, 99
social emotional learning (SEL), 104–106, 108–109
social skills, 103
social story, 78–79, 108
solid teamwork, 42, 132, 146

special education services and programs, 19
special education teachers, 34
splinter skills, 94
strength-based model, 15–16, 41, 146
student empowerment, 42, 55, 81, 111, 131, 146

task analysis, 55–56, 146
teacher preparation programs, 4, 89
teaching assistants, 25
theory of mind, 74
token economy system, 135
twice-exceptional (2E), 23

UDL. *See* universal design for learning
unintentional barriers, 37

United States Department of Education, 17, 19, 24
universal design for learning (UDL), 21, 51–53, 55, 145
unlearning, 36–38, 42, 145

visual supports, 73–74, 102, 111–112
voice and choice, 42, 138, 146–147

welcome, 6–7
West Music, 55, 72
whole language activities, 99
Wilkinson, Lee A, 127–128

Yale Center for Emotional Intelligence, 106
Yoshino, Kenji, 6

About the Author

Brian J. Wagner-Yeung (he/him/his), a music educator and classically trained cellist, is a frequently sought-after clinician in the field of accessible music education. Before teaching, he was raised in Long Island, New York, completing a BA and MSED in music education from CUNY Queens College and an advanced certificate in autism spectrum disorders from CUNY Brooklyn College. He has spent his career at New York City Public Schools as an educator. He has mainly taught music in a center-based special education program, working in inclusive settings and a gifted and talented program. He is also an adjunct faculty member at CUNY Brooklyn College, where he has the luxury of preparing preservice undergraduate and graduate educators in accessible and inclusive music education.

He has also taken on multiple leadership roles. He is the neurodiversity and accessibility chairperson for the New York State School Music Association (NYSSMA®). He was previously on the executive board of the Music Educators' Association of New York City (MEANYC). As an independent educational consultant, he has presented workshops and published articles at the local, national, and international levels.

Brian's work focuses on empowering ALL students to find success through making music and giving music educators the resources, strategies, and tools to allow their music classrooms and programs to become accessible for ALL. He aims to give music educators strategies to create a sense of true inclusion and belonging for ALL. His work can be viewed on his website at www.brianwagneryeung.com.

He currently lives in Queens, New York, with his husband.